D1180616

Developing Technical Training: A Structured Approach for the Development of Classroom and Computer-Based Instructional Materials

RUTH COLVIN CLARK

ADDISON-WESLEY PUBLISHING COMPANY, INC.
Reading, Massachusetts   Menlo Park, California   New York
Don Mills, Ontario   Wokingham, England   Amsterdam
Bonn   Sydney   Singapore   Tokyo   Madrid   San Juan

Library of Congress Cataloging-in-Publication Data

Clark, Ruth Colvin.
  Developing technical training.

  Bibliography: p.
  Includes index.
  1. Technology — Study and teaching. 2. Employees,
Training of. I. Title.
T65.C615 1989   607'.1   88-34964
ISBN 0-201-14967-2

Cover design by Hannus Design Associates
Text design by Patricia Dunbar, Dunbar Design
Set in Times Roman by Compset Inc., Beverly, MA

ABCDEFGHIJ-AL-89
First printing, May 1989

In memory of Colonel Oral B. Bolibaugh, M.D., who was a model of professional dedication and perseverance. And to Ruth Allen Bolibaugh, who has consistently encouraged my work.

Contents

Acknowledgments

I wrote this book to make available in a practical format some of the recent instructional design research and models for producing effective training. I have attempted to summarize theory and to illustrate its applications with many examples from diverse training programs. Therefore, I owe acknowledgments both to those whose theoretical work provided the foundation for this book and to those whose instructional materials I have used as illustrations of how to apply the theory.

As to theory, this book reflects the instructional design model of M. David Merrill, one of my mentors during my doctoral work at USC. Having used his content-performance matrix to teach hundreds of technical experts how to design training, I find it provides a succinct and powerful model. Guidelines for the design of textual materials are based on the work of Robert E. Horn and are available in Information Mapping® seminars. These have proven most useful as a methodology for writing highly readable paper-based documentation. Finally, the illustration of instructional methods applied to two media — workbook and computer — is drawn from the instructional method/instructional media distinction of Richard E. Clark.

As to the examples of classroom and computer-based training materials used to illustrate the theory, I thank my students and colleagues who have generously given permission to include their work. Specifically, I am grateful to the Courseware Developers, Linda Faulkner of InterGraph Corp., Karie Jones of General Dynamics, Rick Pinson of Goal Systems International, Barbara Ross of Information Mapping, Janet Thorp of Intel Corp., David Svoboda of Rockwell International, Roger Kreitman of Mantissa Computer Based Training, and my many colleagues at Southern California Edison Company.

Introduction

As business and industry become increasingly dependent on human resources effectively applying complex technologies, training quality must improve. It's my experience that the skills and knowledge employees need can best be provided by technical experts with considerable experience in applying those technologies on the job. This is true in a variety of domains, including information systems, engineering, finance, statistical quality control, and customer service, to name a few. Several barriers impede the delivery of effective training by such experts:

- First, their own technical knowledge makes it difficult for experts to meet the learning needs of novices. They tend to provide courses that are poorly organized, overloaded with information, sometimes unrelated to job needs, and lacking in sufficient learner involvement.

- Second, a very valuable set of instructional tools is inaccessible to experts in various technical domains. This is because most of the tools and models have been developed in universities and not effectively disseminated into industry. There are not enough instructional design professionals to meet the growing demand for effective training. One solution is to provide the basic instructional design tools directly to technical experts to help them develop effective courses.

- Third, there is a pervasive lack of understanding of what high-quality training in the business environment should be. I believe this problem stems from the assumption that all it takes to provide effective training is content expertise.

- Fourth, there is little evaluation of the instructional effectiveness and cost benefit of most training programs. As long as training providers are not held accountable for demonstrable results, they will have neither the incentive nor the basis for improvement.

- Fifth, there is a blurring of instructional delivery media (workbooks, instructors, computers, etc.) with instructional methods.

Instructional research shows that it is the psychological techniques of the training that lead to learning — not the delivery media. To stress that point I have illustrated these psychological techniques as they apply to two delivery media: workbooks for classroom use and computers for self-instructional training. Each chapter will apply the same instructional principles to both.

This book is written primarily for technical experts throughout business and industry who are charged with the development of effective training. It should also prove valuable to training managers, reviewers and evaluators of training materials, computer-based-training authors, technical writers involved in the development of training documentation, and new instructional design professionals with an interest in industrial/business applications.

Now more than ever, American business and industry need effective training to remain competitive. I hope this book will make a contribution to that goal by making the principles of instructional technology accessible to all technical instructors.

Ruth Colvin Clark

PART ONE

The Technology of Training: An Introduction

The Technology of Training

CHAPTER SUMMARY

- Ineffective training is costing business and industry not only the surface investment made in the training events, but the hidden cost of lost opportunity. Employees who are never trained to effectively or fully utilize the technologies of their work or provide effective customer service add up to a tremendous loss in productivity. We can no longer afford to deliver the inadequate training that has characterized much of the past.

- Research in learning psychology conducted over the past few decades has provided a basis for a technology of training. A technology is the application of principles to achieve a practical result. This book is about many of the powerful tools available to you in the emerging new field of Instructional Technology.

- Instructional Technology is built on a systematic model used to plan, design, develop, and evaluate training. The model is Instructional Systems Design (ISD). By using a systematic process to develop your training, you can "guarantee" learning outcomes.

- The ISD model consists of the following stages: needs analysis, task analysis, definition of learning objectives, development of assessment, development of learning materials, try-out with revision, and implementation of the final product.

- All training consists of four major ingredients: the information of the training, the performance outcomes, the instructional methods, and the instructional media.

- The information is the content of the training program and is defined during task analysis. You define the training content by identifying the information and skills required by the job and subtracting the existing knowledge of your target population.

- The performance outcomes describe what the trainees will do with the information you provide. They are defined in learning objectives and should mirror what the trainee will be required to do on the job. The performance outcomes are the basis on which you will evaluate the success of your training program.

- The instructional methods are the "active psychological ingredients" of the training program. They are what cause the learning to occur. Instructional methods are of two types: informational displays and practice with feedback. The informational displays are keyed to the type of content to be trained and the practice exercises are keyed to the learning objectives.

- The instructional media are the delivery devices that "carry" the instructional methods. Research shows one medium to be as effective as any other as long as it can carry the required instructional methods. Media decisions are based on the instructional methods required by your training objectives and cost-benefit analysis.

- Effective classroom instruction is the product of development activities that result in sound learning materials *and* good classroom delivery skills. It is a common but unrealistic expectation that technical experts should develop and deliver effective classroom instruction without time or support.

There is a common and costly myth that if there are ten or fifteen people in a room with an "instructor" at the front using a chalkboard or an overhead projector, something productive called "training" is going on. Many times the training is a wasted event, in that the learners are unable to do anything new or different as a result. In fact, some studies have shown that trainees were better off before the training than afterwards, when they felt confused and inadequate about their own abilities. Exact estimates of training waste are difficult, since training results are so rarely measured that no one really knows for sure what has — or has not — been accomplished.

THE COST OF TRAINING WASTE

The costs of ineffective training are twofold. First, there are the visible dollars invested in instructors, training materials, and employee time. But even more significant are the lost opportunity costs: the hidden costs of employees who have not been given the skills they need to fully utilize the technologies required by their jobs.

A typical lost-opportunity scenario is associated with the development and installation of a new software system. Months, even years, of effort and hundreds of thousands of dollars are invested in the development of the software. Then, sometimes as an afterthought, someone is asked to put together a training package for the users of the system. Because the resulting training is less than optimal, the software ends up underutilized and a portion — sometimes a substantial portion — of the power of the system is never realized. Employees spend hours poring over confusing technical manuals and end up learning enough of the basics from each other to "get by." Over coffee they talk about how much better things were when they had "good old paper and pencils."

This book is written for individuals with technical training assignments. As job skills become increasingly technical, there is a growing and appropriate trend toward using technical experts as trainers. But this brings us to a second costly training myth: the assumption that all it takes for effective training is an instructor who knows the technical content to be taught. This assumption puts an unfair burden on the experts, who are not given adequate support in the preparation and delivery of that training. It is also

FIGURE 1–1 Two Fatal Assumptions About Training that Lead to the Graveyard of Lost Business Opportunity

Fatal Assumption #1:

A room containing 15 employees and an "instructor" at the front means something productive called "training" is going on.

RIP
Product
Knowledge
$2,350,000

Fatal Assumption #2:

All it takes to be an effective trainer is knowledge of the technical information to be trained.

RIP
Customer
System
$1,236,000

unfair to the employees who are supposedly "trained" and later feel demoralized because they can't apply the skills effectively on the job.

Why We Can't Afford Ineffective Technical Training

Four major trends are making the development of the human resource through effective training a greater priority than in the past:

- First, we are becoming increasingly dependent on the use of new technologies, especially information technologies, as routine business tools.

- Second, service industries continue to grow. By their nature, their success will depend on the quality of service delivered by their employees. This quality of service will not occur spontaneously — training will be needed.

- Third, an elderly population that will be increasing over the next decades requires organizations to think now about how to efficiently transfer a large skill reserve to replace a growing number of retirees.

- Fourth, the basic skill levels of public education graduates at both the high school and college levels continue to decline. Business and industry will need to provide opportunities to adults to acquire skills that in the past were associated with certificates and degrees from educational institutions.

As we move into the 21st century, the development of the human resource can no longer receive less than top priority in any organization determined to remain competitive. In fact, where once the major corporate investment was in capital, we will see an increasing dependency on a skilled human resource for business success.

If you are a technical expert, you are already a valuable resource for your skills and knowledge. But learn to transmit your expertise to others effectively and efficiently and you quadruple your value. Follow the guidelines in this book and your training will be effective, allowing employees to fully utilize the skills you teach and to feel more confident about their work. Furthermore, if you follow the guidelines for measuring training outcomes, you will know — not just guess at — your training results.

The Technology of Training

In the past few decades training has become a technology. A technology is the application of scientific principles to achieve a practical and predictable result. That means the guidelines provided here go beyond a collection of experiences of what seems to work. They are instead based on research results from learning psychology. The principles guiding the design of instructional materials have been incorporated into a new field called *Instructional Technology*.

Instructional Technology provides a systematic approach to planning, developing, and evaluating training. It also offers a set of guidelines that will help you package your technical knowledge in a form that makes it most learnable by your trainees. This book is written primarily for technical experts who are responsible for training. Little or no formal background in training is assumed.

In this chapter I will provide a context for the rest of the book by briefly describing:

• An overview of the Instructional Development Process
• The Four Ingredients of Instruction

INSTRUCTIONAL SYSTEMS DEVELOPMENT: AN OVERVIEW

Out of large-scale engineering projects of the mid-20th century, systematic processes for planning, designing, and building products were born. In the production of complex products such as space stations and airplanes, it was discovered that front-end planning and design saved back-end grief in the actual production effort. More recently, data-processing specialists adopted a similar model called the Systems Life Cycle for the design of complex software. By spending up-front time in analysis and design, they can avoid many mistakes and much extra work during the actual construction of the software. Likewise, in the design of instructional products, a systematic process has proved much more effective than starting right off producing learning materials. Used extensively by the military for training, *Instructional Systems Design* (ISD) methodologies have been widely adopted by many business and industrial training organizations. Several texts on ISD are referenced in the bibliography, but for our purposes a quick overview of the model will serve. If you are familiar with the ISD model, continue on to the section on the Four Ingredients of Instruction on page 12.

Figure 1–2 illustrates a typical ISD model. Note the four major phases: *analysis and design, development, evaluation,* and *implementation.* The analysis and design phase, which can take up to 50% of the total project effort, includes stages of *needs assessment, task analysis, instructional objectives,* and *assessment.* The next section will describe each stage briefly.

Needs Assessment

Sometimes a solution such as "we need a training program" is decided on before the problem has been defined. During needs assessment you determine whether training is, in fact, the appropriate solution. We know that training will solve problems that relate to knowledge and skill deficiencies on the part of the employee. Thus, training is clearly indicated when employees are new or when new technologies or procedures are introduced to an existing work force.

Using Needs Assessment to Identify Appropriate Solutions

Suppose you faced the following real-life problem. Customers were complaining that telephone service agents were rude. It was assumed that a customer-courtesy training program was needed. However, during the needs assessment, it was noted that agents were monitored, and rewarded based on the number of customer calls they processed during a day. Agents were required to handle at least 120 telephone calls per day and were "counseled" if performance fell below that level. The feedback-and-reward system encouraged abrupt conversations in order to meet the target number of calls. No amount of training would change that behavior as

FIGURE 1–2 Instructional Systems Design

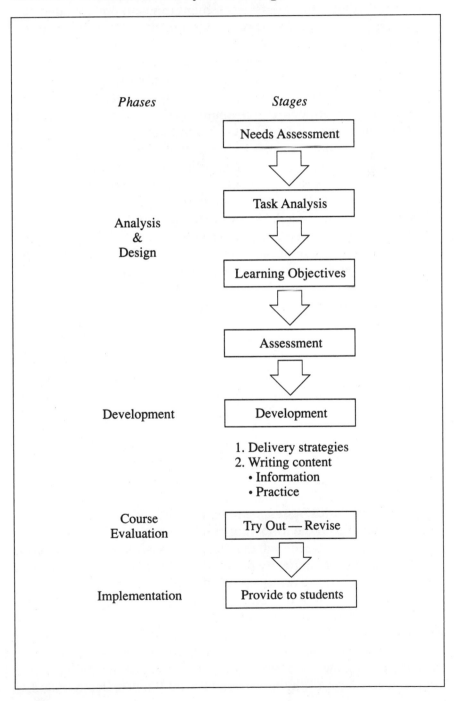

long as rewards were based solely on the number of calls processed. Therefore, the needs assessment report recommended several changes in the performance environment, as well as training.

Using Needs Assessment to Focus Training   Needs assessment can also be used to hone in on *what* training is needed by *whom*. In a large utility, credit agents complained that customer service representatives were mishandling the credit aspects of their job. Customer service representatives did not agree with the credit department's conclusions. To define what, if any, training was needed by whom, a needs assessment study was conducted. All the major credit-related documentation generated by customer service representatives for a one-week period was collected and evaluated for errors. During the same week questions customer service representatives asked credit agents were recorded and analyzed. As a third check a credit skills test was administered to a sample of both customer service representatives and credit agents. The actual credit documents, the questions asked by customer service representatives, and the items missed on the tests were compared for evidence of common misconceptions.

The test results showed that about 40% of both customer service representatives *and* credit agents needed training on commercial accounts. The documentation evaluations and on-the-job questions confirmed the test results. The needs assessment saved money by narrowing the scope of what needed to be trained as well as who actually needed training.

In summary, the needs assessment stage answers the question, "What are the best solutions to a performance problem and, if training is one solution, who needs training on what?" For more information on needs assessment, consult the bibliography.

Task Analysis

Once you have determined that training is what's needed, your next step is to systematically define the content of the training program. This is done by observing skilled performers, interviewing, or reading documentation relevant to the job. If you are a job expert already, you have much of the knowledge in your head. The problem is that you work on the basis of "unconscious competence". You have used your knowledge and skills for so long that they have become automatic. You will need to invest effort to adopt the mind set of the novice to be sure that you have included everything the unskilled employee needs. How to do this will be described throughout the remaining chapters.

During task analysis you not only identify the knowledge and skill requirements of the job, but you also develop a learner profile which defines the target audience's prior knowledge and skills. By subtracting the existing knowledge and skills from those required by the job, you define the content of the training program. More detail on how to do a task analysis is included in Chapter 8.

Learning Objectives

While you are defining the content of the training program, you also specify what the learners will do with that content by writing clearly stated learning objectives. For example, if the content of your training program was how to change a flat tire, your learning objective would require the trainees to change a tire by the end of the program. The section on the Four Ingredients of Training which follows will describe learning objectives in greater detail.

Assessment

You will need some way to determine that your instruction has been successful. You do this by evaluating how well the trainees have achieved the learning objectives. If your objective stated that trainees would be able to change a flat tire, you would administer an assessment to see that each trainee in fact could change a flat tire at the end of the course. To see if your objectives have been reached, you design tests matched to the objectives. If trainees do well on the tests, you know your instruction has been successful.

Remember I started this chapter by mentioning that most training programs cannot state what results have been achieved. That is because they often have no instructional objectives. Or if objectives are available, there is rarely any attempt to see if they have been reached. Even if the test results are not given back to the trainees, they do provide you with evidence of the success of your training. Each chapter in this book will describe appropriate testing techniques for evaluating your training effectiveness.

Development

Once you have completed task analysis, and written performance objectives, and tests, you are ready to develop the instructional materials. The development phase involves the preparation of any instructional resources to be used by the learners during the training. Such activities as writing out workbooks, practice exercises, case studies, or preparing video- or computer-based lessons are included. This book offers guidelines to help you develop effective instructional materials.

Course Evaluation

Once you have developed a draft of your instructional materials, you will need to try them out. You will always find problems with them. Your directions may be confusing or you may not have enough practice on a particular section. Only by pilot-testing your materials will you discover the problems. You will identify problems by interviewing the pilot group of students *and* by evaluating the assessments you give them during the learning session. Based on what your pilot students tell you and on how they do on the assessments, you will need to revise the materials to resolve the major problems encountered.

Implementation

After the instructional program is revised, it can be implemented on a major scale. This might mean distributing your course over computer to 5,000 learners world-wide or teaching it in the classroom to your own group of learners.

With this overview of the ISD process completed, let's examine the four major ingredients of all training programs and relate them to the ISD model.

THE FOUR INGREDIENTS OF TRAINING

All training programs have four major ingredients: *information, performance outcomes, instructional methods* and *instructional media*. An effective training program carefully accounts for and includes each of these. To illustrate each one, examples from an imaginary course on oral hygiene will be used. Our audience for the course is a group of friendly aliens who are adapting to Earth culture. These aliens are familiar with mouths and teeth but that's about all they know.

1: The Information

It is obvious that all courses include a content to be trained. The content, or course information, is defined and organized during the task analysis stage of the ISD process. The content of the course is decided by looking at both the knowledge and skill requirements of the job and the knowledge and skill levels of the intended training audience. By subtracting the knowledge and skills of the intended audience from those of the job, you can derive final course content.

This sounds easier than it often is. That's why the analysis and design of your courses can consume up to 50% of your total development effort. If you are a technical expert you may be one of the major resources of knowledge and skills. As mentioned above, your major challenge will be to make all that knowledge explicit and get it logically organized.

All course content can be classified as one of five types: *facts, concepts, processes, procedures,* and *principles.* This book is organized around each of these types of content. Thus Chapter 3 deals with how to teach procedures, Chapter 4 with how to teach concepts, and so forth.

As shown in Figure 1–3, our oral hygiene course includes content related to: toothbrushes, knowing how often to brush, and being able to brush correctly. Each of these is a different type of content. "Toothbrush" is an example of a concept while "learning how to brush" would be a procedure.

While the content is important, many technical instructors never get beyond it in their course development. Courses end up as massive dumps of technical data. To avoid this pitfall, ask yourself, "What do you want your learners to do with the content?" The purpose of business training is to give employees capabilities they need to perform their jobs effectively. Therefore, defining what they must *do* with the content is as important as defining the content itself. That brings us to the second ingredient of instruction: the performance outcome.

2: The Performance Outcome

The performance outcome is a clearly defined statement of what the learners will be doing when they have achieved the purpose of the course or lesson. Performance outcomes should mirror what must be done on the job. They are written in the form of learning objectives described above under the ISD model. Each of your lessons will have at least one major learning objective and many will include supporting objectives as well.

Note the performance outcomes for our oral hygiene lesson in Figure 1–4. These sample objectives include a clear action statement, a description of conditions under which the action will take place, and a standard of quality required. The first objective is a

FIGURE 1–3

FOUR INGREDIENTS OF TRAINING: #1

INFORMATION

WHAT FACTS, CONCEPTS, PROCESSES, PROCEDURES
OR PRINCIPLES MUST BE DELIVERED IN THE
TRAINING?

EXAMPLE: ORAL HYGIENE SKILLS

What is a toothbrush?   CONCEPT

How often should you brush your teeth?   FACT

How do you brush your teeth?   PROCEDURE

	REQUIRED		PRIOR
TRAINING CONTENT =	JOB	MINUS	LEARNER
	INFORMATION		KNOWLEDGE

DEFINED DURING TASK ANALYSIS PHASE OF ISD MODEL

FIGURE 1–4

FOUR INGREDIENTS OF TRAINING: #2

PERFORMANCE OUTCOMES

> WHAT MUST THE TRAINEES BE ABLE TO DO AT THE END OF THE TRAINING?

- STATED IN LEARNING OBJECTIVES

- SHOULD MIRROR WHAT THE TRAINEES WILL DO ON THE JOB

EXAMPLE: ORAL HYGIENE SKILLS

Given typical bathroom supplies, the learners will identify the toothbrush, toothpaste, and floss with 100% accuracy.

Given toothbrush, toothpaste, and floss, the learners will brush and floss their teeth following the procedures demonstrated in class.

DEFINED DURING TASK ANALYSIS PHASE OF ISD MODEL

supporting objective, which describes what the student will do to demonstrate that he can identify the concept "toothbrush." The second is the major lesson objective, which describes what the student will do when he has learned the procedure of brushing his teeth.

Notice that these performance outcomes include an *observable* action verb. They avoid use of words such as "know" or "understand." Why? Because the performance outcome will be used to measure the effectiveness of the training. Suppose your outcome was "the students will know what a toothbrush is." How will you or the students determine that they "know"? An observable action, something we can see right away, is required. So we ask the student to pick out the toothbrush from an assortment of common bathroom supplies.

The learning objective is important because it will provide a guideline for designing practice exercises and evaluating lesson success. As illustrated in Figure 1–5, the learning objectives, practice exercises, and test items are like jigsaw puzzle pieces. Each matches the others to make the training internally consistent. To find out more about learning objectives, consult the bibliography.

3: The Instructional Methods

This book is about instructional methods. Once you have identified both the content and the performance outcomes, you are ready to start developing the instruction. When developing instructional

FIGURE 1–5 Matching Test Items and Practice to Learning Objectives

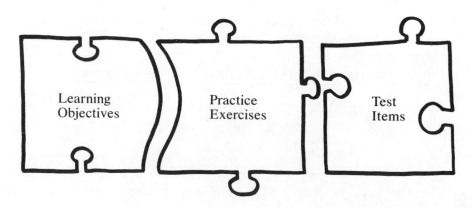

materials, you will want to make use of a proven set of tools known as instructional methods. These methods are the psychologically active ingredients of your training program that will best promote learning.

As you can see in Figure 1–6, instructional methods are of two types: informational displays, and practice exercises with feedback. The type of informational displays you will need depends on the type of content. Displays for facts are different from those needed for concepts or procedures. To teach the concept of toothbrush, the displays needed are a *definition, examples,* and *non-examples*. Each chapter in this book will describe the informational displays needed for the various types of content and show you how to format them for workbooks and computer screens.

The best practice exercise will match the learning objective, as in Figure 1–5. A well-written learning objective will tell you how to design the practice. For example, the performance outcome that states that the learner will be able to identify a toothbrush among an assortment of bathroom tools tells you to give the students practice picking out toothbrushes from a variety of common bathroom supplies. Ways of designing practice will be described in each chapter, with examples drawn from a number of successful training courses.

As mentioned earlier, this book will illustrate the use of these instructional methods for two media: workbook and computer. This brings us to the last ingredient of instruction: the delivery media.

4: The Instructional Media

The instructional methods must be delivered through a medium or a mix of media. In a typical classroom the media mix includes: the instructor, a workbook, overhead transparencies, flip-charts, and perhaps a video. When designing computer-based training, the major medium is the computer, supplemented at times by print materials. In Figure 1–7, for example, the media used for our toothbrushing course include an instructor, a workbook, and a video.

INSTRUCTIONAL MEDIA: WHICH ONES ARE THE BEST?

B. F. Skinner once wrote about teaching machines, "Obviously the machine itself does not teach. It simply brings the student into contact with the person who composed the material it presents. It is a

FIGURE 1–6

FOUR INGREDIENTS OF TRAINING: #3

INSTRUCTIONAL METHODS

WHAT INSTRUCTIONAL METHODS (TECHNIQUES)
ARE NEEDED TO DELIVER THE INFORMATION AND
ACHIEVE PERFORMANCE OUTCOMES?

- INFORMATIONAL DISPLAYS
- PRACTICE EXERCISES WITH FEEDBACK

EXAMPLE: HOW TO IDENTIFY THE TOOTHBRUSH

CONCEPT

Definition: A toothbrush is a small brush with
bristles at end and a long handle
usually made out of plastic used
exclusively for brushing teeth.

Informational
Displays:

BRISTLES   HANDLE

Example:

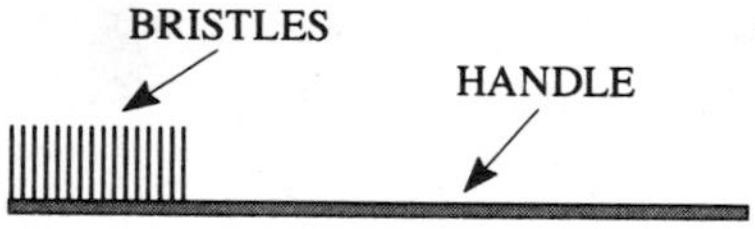

Non-example:

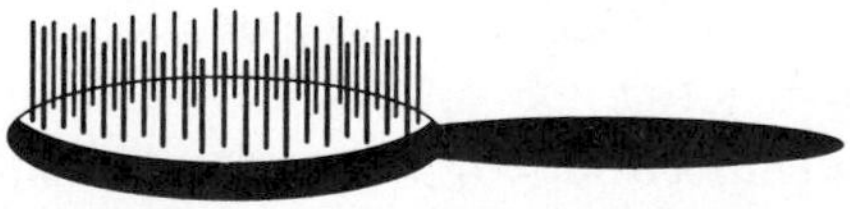

Practice   On the table is an assortment of bathroom supplies.
Exercise: Pick out the toothbrush.

DEFINED DURING THE DEVELOPMENT PHASE
OF THE ISD MODEL

FIGURE 1–7

FOUR INGREDIENTS OF TRAINING: #4

INSTRUCTIONAL MEDIA

> WHAT MEDIA WILL MOST EFFICIENTLY AND
> EFFECTIVELY DELIVER THE REQUIRED
> INSTRUCTIONAL METHODS?

EXAMPLE: ORAL HYGIENE SKILLS

DELIVERY   Instructor
MEDIA:
                  Workbook

                  Video

MEDIA DECISIONS BASED ON:

• Can the media deliver the required instructional methods?

> If you need to provide realistic examples of a sales
> technique, you would need video or live demonstration

• Administrative issues of efficiency

> Location of trainees, available hardware

DEFINED BEFORE/DURING TASK ANALYSIS PHASE

labor-saving device because it can bring one programmer into contact with an indefinite number of students." (*Scientific American,* November 1961) In spite of this early observation, research studies have tried for years to identify the best media. But there are no "best" media. As Skinner stated, the media are passive carriers of the active ingredients of learning — the instructional methods. No one medium is better than another as long as it can carry the required methods. Thus comparisons of courses taught by an instructor with the same courses taught by computer show no differences in learning, provided the same instructional methods are used. For more information on this phenomenon refer to articles in the instructional media section of the bibliography.

Making Your Media Choices

Media choices are best made by selecting the most cost-effective media that will carry the instructional methods required. For example, effective sales training requires examples of successful exchanges between account representatives and customers. Two media could carry these examples: a classroom instructor or a video tape. Often a video is used because it can provide effective examples time after time, which may be difficult to guarantee when a variety of different instructors deliver the training.

If you needed to teach a course on statistical quality control, you could use either an instructor with a workbook or a computer. If the training were consistently designed, learning outcomes would be equivalent, and your preference would depend on an analysis of cost benefit. If the course was to be delivered to 5,000 employees who work with computers already and are located internationally, it would probably be cheaper to use computer-based delivery than to pay the expenses of sending instructors and/or students to courses.

Technical Instructors As Developers and Delivery Media

The confusion between media and methods is at the root of another inaccurate assumption: that instructors can simultaneously develop and deliver effective training. All too often, technical experts are asked to teach a course on very short notice. As a result there is minimal lesson development, under the assumption that the delivery process will generate effective instruction automatically.

FIGURE 1-8 Effective Instruction: Development Plus Delivery

Fatal Assumption #3:

The technical expert can simultaneously develop and deliver effective training.

RIP
Better
Customer
Service
$15,364,280

More often than not, the result is wasted training time. Successful training requires an up-front development effort, independent of the effort that must be put into delivering the course.

To summarize, we have identified four major components that need to be separately addressed in your training program. During task analysis you will define the training *content* and the *performance outcomes*. During development you will use the right *instructional methods* to communicate the content and achieve the performance outcomes. The final training will be delivered via the mix of *media* which can carry the instructional methods and offer greatest cost benefit.

CHECK YOUR UNDERSTANDING

To see if you can distinguish the Four Ingredients of Instruction try the practice exercise on page 237.

PREVIEW OF CHAPTER 2

Chapter 2 will provide an introduction to structured lesson design. It will include an overview of a typical technical lesson, introduce the educational taxonomy that serves as the foundation for Chapters 3–7, and describe the rationale for the text formats to be presented.

An Introduction to Structured Lesson Design

CHAPTER SUMMARY

- Technical lessons include four major sections: an introduction, background information, the key lesson skill, and a summary.

- The introduction should include a statement of the purpose and benefits of the skills to be learned, the context of the lesson, the lesson objective, and an outline of the lesson content.

- The background information and key lesson skill sections use instructional methods consisting of information displays interspersed with practice exercises. Chapters 3–7 will describe the design of displays and practice exercises in detail.

- The instructional methods included in Chapters 3–7 are based on the Content-Performance Matrix, an educational classification system developed by M. David Merrill. The matrix provides a succinct, practical, research-based model for assignment of instructional methods.

- The Content Performance Matrix includes five types of content: facts, concepts, processes, procedures, and principles. Each content type can be processed at two levels of performance: remember and apply. These will be described in detail in Chapters 3–7.

- The information formats matched to the types of content illustrated in Chapters 3–7 for textual displays are based on guidelines developed by Robert E. Horn. These formats promote fast access and retrieval of technical information, and give your technical documentation a consistent appearance.

- Research shows improved learning outcomes result from providing learners with a detailed set of course notes as suggested in this book. Cost-benefit issues associated with the additional development effort involved are discussed.

In Chapter 1, I summarized the Instructional Systems Design (ISD) model and described the four ingredients of all training programs: information (or content), performance outcomes, instructional methods, and the media used to deliver the methods. This book is about ingredient number three, the instructional methods, the psychological tools you can use to generate the learning outcomes that best fit job needs. Ways to format these methods for two media — workbooks for classroom instruction and computers for computer-based self-instructional training (CBT) — will be described in Chapters 3–7.

Before getting into the details, this chapter will set the context by introducing some of the underlying principles for structured lesson design. In particular this chapter will include:

- a generic structure for technical lessons
- an overview of the Content-Performance Matrix, which forms the basis for the instructional methods to be presented
- an introduction to the structured formats recommended for display of information, both in workbooks and on computer screens.

THE ANATOMY OF A LESSON

Figure 2–1 illustrates a high-level structure that you can use for the development of all lessons. It provides a consistent framework into which you can incorporate the instructional methods needed for learning. Using a structured approach has several advantages. If more than one instructor is developing a course, it will look like one course rather than a mixture of several different courses. If a

FIGURE 2–1 High-Level Lesson Structure

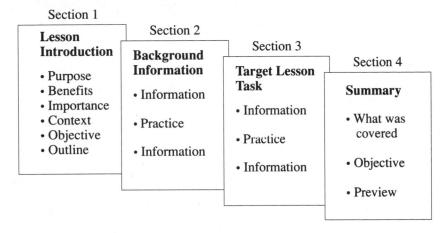

series of lessons is built by different authors or even the same author over time, consistency can be maintained. Once you are familiar with the structured lesson-design formats, you will save a lot of development time by plugging in the formats that fit the overall structure of your lessons. Because the structure incorporates research-based principles, you can be assured of providing effective instructional materials.

Lessons using this structured approach have four major sections:

1. introduction
2. supporting information
3. target skill(s) of the lesson
4. summary

Sections 2 and 3 make up the body of the lesson. Section 3 teaches the major skill or task of that lesson. Section 2 teaches all the information needed to understand that major skill or task. Both sections include blocks of information interspersed with practice exercises. Chapters 3–7 will illustrate these information displays and practice exercises. For now, let's take a brief look at each of the four sections of a technical lesson.

The Lesson Introduction

A lesson introduction typically uses one to two pages in a workbook or five to ten screens in a computer-based training lesson. An effective introduction both orients and motivates trainees. You can refer to the "How to Brush Your Teeth" lesson introduction illus-trated in Figure 2–2 as I summarize the important features. The introduction to the lesson should include:

- a statement of the purpose, benefits, and importance of the les-son, to motivate the learner
- an orienting statement that relates how this lesson fits into the course structure
- a statement of the lesson objective(s)
- an outline of the material to be included in the lesson.

In computer-based training lessons, add an estimate of lesson completion time (since the computer gives no physical clues as to lesson length) and some learner-control options to allow the stu-dent to choose topics of interest. Learner control will be described in Chapter 9.

FIGURE 2–2 Sample Lesson Introduction

HOW TO BRUSH YOUR TEETH	
Introduction	In this lesson you will learn the correct procedure for brushing your teeth. This is an especially important skill, because without regular cleaning teeth tend to deteriorate — a process called decay.
	In the last lesson you learned about appropriate grooming of hair for both men and women. This lesson on toothbrushing also applies to both sexes.
Objective	At the end of this lesson you will:
	• pick out a toothbrush and toothpaste from other normal bathroom supplies
	• follow the recommended steps to brush your teeth
Outline	This lesson includes the following topics:
	Why Brush? — The Process of Tooth Decay What is a Toothbrush? What is Toothpaste? When to Brush Practice # 1 How to Brush Your Teeth Practice # 2 Summary of Lesson

The Lesson Body

Following the introduction, the body of the lesson includes two sections: the *supporting information* and the *target skill*. I refer to the supporting information included in Section 2 as the "hidden mental skills," which include all the technical terms and facts related to the major lesson skill. For example, the target skill of our toothbrushing lesson is "how to brush your teeth." But, in order to brush, you would need to know about toothbrushes, toothpaste, and when to brush. Technical experts often leave out these hidden mental skills because they forget that novices do not have them. Instead, they jump right into the major skill, and trainees get confused by the use of background terminology and facts which were never explained.

The third section of your lesson teaches the major task or skill to be trained and includes both information displays and practice exercises. The major task will usually be based on either a procedure which is described in the next chapter or on guidelines derived from principles described in Chapter 7.

The Lesson Summary

Last, you include a brief lesson summary, which includes a condensed presentation of the key information points and a reminder of the lesson objective to focus trainee attention on their achievement of the performance outcomes of the lesson. It might also include a preview leading into the next lesson.

Lesson Structure for Workbooks Versus CBT

The structure described above is followed for CBT lessons as well as textual materials. The major difference will be the spacing of information with practice within the sections. If the computer lesson is intended to be self-instructional it must both maintain learner interest and support immediate acquisition of knowledge. Relatively small amounts of information, coupled with more frequent learner responses, are essential. While both classroom and computer training must be highly interactive, the instructor can maintain attention and use the workbook to supplement human memory for relatively longer periods of time than can the computer. Therefore, as we discuss design of CBT lessons you will see small chunks of information followed by more frequent interspersal of practice questions.

EDUCATIONAL TAXONOMIES AND INSTRUCTIONAL METHODS

Chapters 3–7 will focus on the detailed instructional methods that fit into the lesson structure described above. In Chapter 1, I made the point that these methods are based on research guidelines from learning psychology. In this section I will introduce the *Content-Performance Matrix,* the classification system or taxonomy on which the methods in Chapters 3–7 are based. First I will give a brief historical background into the evolution and significance of educational taxonomies. If this background information is not of interest to you, bypass this section and go right to the overview of the Content-Performance Matrix on page 29.

Educational Taxonomies and Technology

Every significant technology, from medicine to engineering, has evolved through similar stages. They began as crafts, with designated practitioners. The barbers who served as medical practitioners in past centuries each had their own idiosyncratic approach to their craft. Before formalization or scientific principles, any one approach was as good as any other.

In the next stage, commonalities are observed and grouped into classification systems known as taxonomies. Research studies validate the usefulness of the taxonomy. In medicine, systematic recorded observations noted commonalities in symptoms which were gradually classified as diseases. This stage symbolizes a major transition from craft to technology. Documented objective categories represent the beginning of the formalization of knowledge and the application of principles.

Bloom's Taxonomy   One of the first taxonomies of learning was presented by Benjamin Bloom in the 1950s in a model which included three major types of learning outcomes: *cognitive* (or intellectual), *affective* (or attitudinal), and *psychomotor* (or physical). This was the first time a formal systematic distinction was made between such diverse goals as learning how to ride a bike (psychomotor), how to solve a long-division problem (cognitive), and how to generate commitment to a democratic form of government (affective).

A useful taxonomy will group learning goals to suggest different ways each should be taught. In medicine, a valid grouping of diseases categorizes symptoms by the treatments they will respond to, because there are commonalities in underlying causes. In education, any powerful taxonomy would need to include categories which validly suggest differences in the ways the learning outcomes could be achieved.

Gagne's Conditions of Learning   To this end, Robert Gagne, in his 1965 book *The Conditions Of Learning,* introduced a more prescriptive taxonomy than Bloom's. He not only included five types of major different learning outcomes but also described the *conditions* under which each is acquired. His work was one of the first that attempted to describe how instruction should be designed to provide the conditions required by different types of learning outcomes. From the late '50s into the '70s these conditions were expanded by a number of research studies that resulted in improved methodologies for teaching different types of content.

Merrill's Content-Performance Matrix   Building on the work of Gagne and the other research, M. David Merrill produced the taxonomy which, adapted somewhat, forms the basis for this book. I have found that his model, the Content-Performance Matrix, provides technical experts with a very effective and succinct basis for designing effective instructional materials. To find out more about the original model, read the chapters by Merrill in Reigeluth's books referenced in the bibliography.

The Content-Performance Matrix: An Introduction

As shown in Figure 2–3, the matrix is two-dimensional with five types of content along the horizontal axis and two levels of performance along the vertical. Recall from Chapter 1 that two of the ingredients of instruction are the information, or content, and the performance outcome. The information you teach can be classified as facts, concepts, processes, procedures, or principles. Your performance outcomes can be written at a remember or application level.

A remember outcome requires very little mental processing as it asks the trainee to recall or recognize information in an untransformed state. For example, you might ask your trainees to "list the commands needed to access customer records." To accomplish this task, the trainee memorizes the commands as presented in the

FIGURE 2–3 The Content-Performance Matrix: An Educational Taxonomy

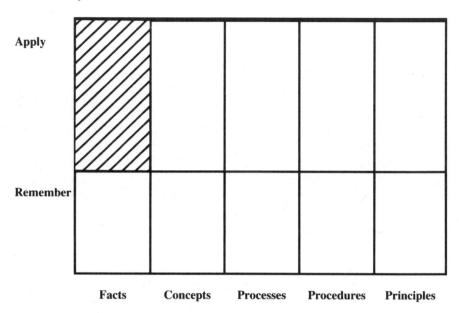

instructional materials. However, being able to list the commands does not insure that the trainee can actually access the customer records.

The bulk of your training should be targeted toward the application level which requires the trainee to use the information the way it will be used on the job. An application-level version of the above objective would ask your trainees to "enter the commands to access the customer records." Your instruction should provide a job card listing the steps and get the trainees to apply them as soon as possible. Detailed definitions of all five types of content and the two levels of performance will be presented in the following chapters.

How the Matrix Helps Develop Training   The power of the model is the matching of instructional methods to each of the cells in the matrix. For example, if you are teaching a concept such as "toothbrush" at the application level, there are certain informational displays and practice exercises you will need to use. An example of these particular displays is shown in Figure 1–6. If you need to teach factual information at the remember level, there are different guidelines to follow. The information displays are keyed to the type of content involved.

Practice exercises are designed according to the level of performance. You will design a different practice exercise if you want your trainees to remember a concept than if you want them to apply it. Note the practice exercise used to support the application of the toothbrush concept in Figure 1–6. In summary, the matrix provides the basis for rules you can use to develop training materials that work. This book is about those rules.

Chapters 3 through 7 define each of the five types of content and show you how to provide information displays and practice exercises — appropriate for workbook or computer delivery — at the remember and application levels. Although the *methods* will be the same for workbook and computer, the *formats* will change to accommodate the differences between 8½″-by-11″ pages and 80-line-by-20-column computer screens. In this final section, I will introduce the structured formats to be presented in the following chapters.

STRUCTURED WRITING TECHNIQUES

If you have never seen structured writing formats before, some of the layouts will look quite strange at first. For example, look at the introduction to the toothbrush lesson in Figure 2–2. Note the use of marginal labels and lines to separate text. These are some of the most visible differences you will note in the structured materials. These formats are not arbitrary in their design. Research on layout and display of text has shown these to be especially advantageous to speed access and retrieval of technical information.

Test Your Speed When Reading Structured Writing   To test this out on yourself, try a little experiment. On page 33 in Figure 2–4 you will see a typical business memo. Before looking at it, use a watch with a second hand to time yourself. Ready? Now read that memo to find out the new business position of Jack Spotter. Note how long it takes you. Now repeat the experiment with the same memo reformatted in a structured style, located on the next page. Once again, time yourself. This time find out the new business position of Janice Moreland. Compare your information-access times. When doing this in training courses, I find a typical 40–60 second advantage in retrieval of information in Version 2 over Version 1. Multiply this by the amount of technical information buried in typical business documentation to appreciate the value of the structured writing methodologies.

Text Design Research

Research on text design shows that the retrieval and recall advantages result from:

- effective organization of related chunks of information
- identification of that information by headings and labels. While my examples use marginal labels, research has shown that embedded labels are equally effective.
- elimination of unnecessary words by use of tables
- use of white space to separate information

Besides the readability advantages, the structured formats provide a detailed shell you can use to give your instruction visual and instructional consistency. By verifying that the correct displays match the type of content being taught, you can quickly validate the effectiveness of the instructional materials.

The different content types and associated information-layout techniques in this book were originally developed by Robert E. Horn in the mid-1960s. Horn's method, which is taught in Information Mapping® seminars, is a comprehensive set of tools and techniques for identifying what needs to be communicated, organizing and managing large amounts of complex information, and presenting the information in consistent formats supported by human-factors research.

Because the computer screen is smaller than the page and offers additional display possibilities with color and movement, the formats are modified somewhat from those seen in the text examples. Note that for both text and computer screens the use of ample background space and distinctive labels improves readability and information retrieval.

Detailed Versus Outline Notes: Research Guidelines

Typical business and industrial training sessions use an outline approach, in which the instructor summarizes the major points to be presented in brief statements. The instructor then lectures from

FIGURE 2–4 Before — A Typical Business Memo

DATE: April 3, 1987
TO: All Employees
FROM: Oliver Castle, President

Company Reorganization

As you probably already know, several business factors have affected us this year including the expansion of imports from the foreign market, union difficulties and problems with the development of new components, especially in the personal system products. Therefore, management has assessed our entire company and its operations with a view to finding a way for the organization to improve profits and increase long-term efficiency. Some of our departments have been growing and shrinking without much rhyme or reason, and before this we had not made the effort to take a really hard look at what we were doing. Instead, we were patching things up here and there with the aim of eliminating duplication when we could and pulling together groups that belong together functionally.

Now we are announcing a major reorganization to take effect on April 19. We will announce the details on April 12, such as when the desks will be moved and when new managers will hold meetings with various employees to whom the information is pertinent. We will also, at that time, distribute a complete schedule setting forth who will be working for whom. In the meantime, we are announcing the following changes so the managers in charge of the affected divisions and departments can prepare for the reorganization.

Don Smyth will assume duties as Director of the new Operations Division, leaving his present post as Manager of Equipment and Supplies. Janice Moreland will move from Vice President for Research to Vice President of the new division. Jack Spotter will be the new Vice President of Product Development, moving from his position as Assistant Director of Research. These changes in department managerial positions will take place on April 5.

Jerry Franklin and Marsha Magary will become Assistant Director of Research and Assistant Director of Operations, respectively, from their current positions as Assistant Director of Finance and Manager of Accounting. Employees directly affected will be informed by April 10 by their managers about whether they will be moving. In most cases, employees who work for the managers named above will stay with their manager.

FIGURE 2–5 **After — Same Memo Using Structured Writing Method**

DATE: April 3, 1987
TO: All Employees
FROM: Oliver Castle, President

SUBJECT: TWO NEW DIVISIONS ANNOUNCED

Background	As you know, several business factors have affected us this year, including • the expansion of import trade from foreign markets • union difficulties, and • problems with the development of new components, especially in the personal system products. Therefore, management has reorganized the company to improve profitability and increase long-term efficiency.
New divisions added	Effective April 19, we will add two new divisions: • Product Development, and • Operations. All other divisions will remain the same.
Management changes	The following people have been promoted effective April 5.

NAME	PRESENT POSITION	NEW POSITION
Don Smyth	Manager, Equipment and Supplies	Director, Operations
Janice Moreland	V.P., Research	V.P., Operations
Jack Spotter	Asst. Director, Research	V.P., Product Development
Jerry Franklin	Asst. Director, Finance	Asst. Director, Research
Marsha Magary	Manager, Accounting	Asst. Director, Operations

Impact on employees	Most employees who work for these managers will remain with their current managers. If the changes will affect you, your manager will notify you by April 10.
Effective dates	The effective dates for these changes are as follows: • April 5 — Management changes • April 10 — Employee notification of relocation • April 12 — Details of reorganization announced • April 19 — Reorganization effective.

FIGURE 2–6 **The Outline Notes Version**

Direction of Questions

- Rhetorical
  — A question that you intend to answer yourself
  — A good way to maintain interest during lecture

- Group
  — A question directed to all attendees
  — A non-threatening way to initiate interaction

- Targeted
  — A question directed toward a particular attendee
  — Best way to sustain attention during lecture
  — For maximum interaction, pose question as follows
    — Question
    — Pause (at least 3 seconds)
    — Call on attendee

transparencies that list these major outline points. Trainees take notes on paper copies of the transparencies. Figure 2–6 illustrates a typical example. In this book it is suggested that you prepare more detailed written student materials. Figure 2–7 shows the previous outline fleshed out using the structured writing techniques to be presented in this book. Obviously this more detailed approach will take more time to develop than the outlines. Is it worth it?

Recent research by Kenneth Kiewra and Bernard Frank compared the learning outcomes among students who either took notes without any material from the instructor, took notes based on outlines such as those shown in Figure 2–6, or who were provided with detailed notes. The research concluded that "generally, being provided with detailed notes produced higher factual achievement than did the review of either personal notes or skeletal notes, thereby making detailed notes the best means of external storage." It is interesting that the improved learning was achieved on delayed tests, but not on immediate ones, indicating that detailed notes provide an improved source of information for later reference. The research by Kiewra and Frank is referenced under "Text Design" in the bibliography.

Writing detailed notes provides your learners with an accurate

FIGURE 2–7 The Detailed Notes Version

EFFECTIVE QUESTIONING TECHNIQUES

Introduction One of your major tools for holding trainee attention is the question. This section will discuss different types of questions and provide techniques for asking questions and responding.

Type of Questions

Questions are of two major types:

• Open-Ended — these questions do not have a right or wrong answer. They typically ask for an opinion or experience.

What advantages did you see to using that software?

• Close-Ended — these questions have a definite answer.

How many characters can be entered in that field?

Direction of Questions

Questions can be directed in five ways:

• Group — these questions are open for anyone to answer

• Targeted — these questions are asked of a specific individual

• Relay — these questions originate with a trainee and are bounced back to a different trainee

• Reverse — These questions are thrown back to the asker

• Rhetorical — questions you answer yourself

---

record of information for future reference. It also gives them an opportunity to concentrate on the lecture and add their own tailored comments, rather than devote energy to writing down the information as you speak it. Finally, for complex technical training information which is often presented in relatively short periods of time, the more detailed notes compensate for inadequate time and/ or the fast pace of the instructor. Thus, effective results can be achieved even if the delivery techniques are less than optimum.

It is clear that learning results are improved by detailed notes.

FIGURE 2–8 **A Compromise to Detailed Notes**

EFFECTIVE QUESTIONING TECHNIQUES

Introduction

Type of Questions	Questions are of 2 major types:		
		Definition	Examples
	Open ended:		
	Closed ended:		
Direction of Questions	Questions can be directed in 5 ways:		
		Definition	Examples
	Group:		
	Targeted:		
	Relay:		
	Reverse:		
	Rhetorical:		

Still, you will need to consider the cost benefit of the additional effort in terms of other factors, including the number of trainees and the importance and longevity of the information you are presenting. To take extremes, a one-time course for ten employees on relatively unimportant tasks would warrant less effort than a long-term course for 1,000 on critical tasks. Although this book will illustrate development of detailed instructional materials, a compromise would be to provide complete notes on critical skills, and the page headings and marginal labels for less essential information, as in Figure 2–8.

By evaluating the results of your training through testing you can demonstrate the effectiveness of whatever approach you use. It is ultimately a management issue to decide on the cost benefit of more and less effective training techniques. But until someone evaluates the outcomes and presents alternative approaches, there is no basis to show the benefits of improved training techniques.

PREVIEW OF THE REMAINDER OF THE BOOK

The key to effective technical training lies in the use of the right instructional methods to help learners achieve the performance outcomes relevant to their jobs. These methods include information displays and design of practice exercises. This book will describe and illustrate the major instructional methods that research has proven most effective.

Chapters 3–7 will take each of the five content types and present the information displays and practice exercises required to effectively instruct them, along with testing techniques you can use to be sure your trainees have acquired them. Chapter 3 will begin with one of the most common target-lesson tasks: the procedure. Chapters 4 and 5 will describe how to teach the most common forms of information to accompany procedures: concepts and facts. Chapter 6 will describe processes which frequently provide job-related contextual information. Chapter 7 will present the second type of common target lesson tasks: principles. Having described all the types of content, Chapter 8 will return to the issue of how to define the content that goes into your lessons and, having defined it, how to organize it. Finally, Chapter 9 will address some issues of computer-based training that are not faced in design of classroom textual materials.

To give you additional opportunities to process what you are reading, brief practice exercises adapted from my workshop are referenced in most of the chapters. The exercises and answers will be found in the appendix.

Having taught workshops on how to design training to hundreds of technical experts, I have attempted in this book to summarize the major guidelines which I have found to work well for them. Many of the topics mentioned could themselves become entire books. I have developed a bibliography of recent books and articles on some of these topics for further reading.

PART TWO

Designing Training for Five Basic Content Types

The Context-Performance Matrix: Procedures

	Facts	Concepts	Processes	Procedures	Principles
Apply	///////			Perform the Procedure *Log onto the Computer*	
Remember				Remember the Steps *List the Steps to Log onto the Computer*	

C H A P T E R   3

How to Teach Procedures

CHAPTER SUMMARY

- A procedure is a series of clearly defined steps which result in achievement of a job task. Procedures that consist of a single stream of steps are linear procedures. Branched procedures consist of two or more alternative linear procedures which are selected on the basis of clearly specified criteria.

- Procedures can be learned at the remember level by memorizing the steps. This is not a recommended approach. Procedures can be learned at the application level by doing the procedures.

- Information displays for teaching procedures include action and decision tables in training manuals and displays of steps in a window or lower-section of the screen in computer-based training (CBT).

- Classroom practice should get employees to the application level quickly by providing follow-along demonstrations and exercises that require the employee to perform the procedure.

- CBT practice of procedures should be closely linked to the information displays by moving from guided to unguided simulations.

- Evaluation of learning should be based on performance tests. During the performance test the instructor observes the employee doing the procedure, using a checklist to eval-

uate the quality of the performance. CBT can use unguided, scored simulations or instructor-led laboratory follow-up sessions.

The purpose of virtually all business/industrial training is to teach employees the skills they need to successfully perform their job tasks. This means teaching them tasks that are based either on procedures or on the application of principles. Chapter 7 will describe how to teach principle-based tasks.

This chapter will show you the most efficient way to train procedures. After describing the types of procedures to be trained, I'll discuss how they can be learned at the remember and application levels. Then I'll illustrate how to provide the information displays and practice exercises that best teach procedural skills, both in training manuals for classroom instruction and on screens for computer-based training (CBT). Last, I'll discuss how to evaluate how well your trainees have learned the procedures.

WHAT IS A PROCEDURE?

A procedure is a series of clearly defined steps which result in achievement of a job task. Some typical examples include: logging onto a computer, doing preventative maintenance on a pump, and taking a customer order. Procedures are done more or less the same way each time and can be clearly specified in a step-by-step format. A large proportion of all business/industrial training is procedurally based, training employees to perform the tasks to do their jobs efficiently, effectively, and safely. Effective training of procedures is therefore a critical skill for the training developer or instructor.

Types of Procedures

There are two basic types of procedures: *linear* and *branched*. Linear procedures are made up of clearly specified observable steps which are generally undertaken in the same sequence each time. You can document the procedure by watching an experienced employee do the task. Logging onto a computer or doing preventative maintenance are two examples of linear procedures.

Branched procedures are made up of two or more linear procedural sequences. A branched procedure is like a flow chart. The employee must make a decision which will lead her to continue along sequence X or sequence Y. You have to find out the *criteria* of the decision by asking an experienced employee why they were doing X instead of Y. How to establish credit in a new customer is a branched procedure. When the credit representative takes the order, he asks the customer a series of questions. Based on the customer's responses, the representative assigns a credit code to the customer and may or may not require a deposit. The credit representative makes the decision based on a clearly specified set of company criteria. For example, if the customer owns his home or has an employment reference, a credit code of 3 might be assigned and the deposit waived.

Simple troubleshooting sequences are also based on a branched procedure. Depending on the symptoms of equipment failure, a technician might first try one of three tests to isolate the problem. Depending on the results of these tests, a further series of tests would be conducted, followed by repair of the equipment.

Branched procedures are made up of two or more linear procedures sequenced after a decision point. In other words, the employee is making a decision in order to take some specific action. For example, if the customer is assigned a credit code of 5, ask for a $200 deposit. Or if the start-up mechanism shows a fault, replace or repair the component.

CHECK YOUR UNDERSTANDING

To be sure you can identify linear and branched procedures, try the short exercise on page 239.

Learning Procedures at the Remember and Application Levels

As mentioned in Chapter 2, the five types of content can be learned at two levels: remember and application. In order to apply a procedure the first time, the employee needs access to the steps, but memorization is generally a waste of time. You want the employee to *do* the procedure — not memorize steps. Therefore, quickly move your instruction to the application level. In the next section I will discuss and illustrate how to teach procedures so that your trainees quickly begin to apply the new skills.

Writing Procedure Learning Objectives at the Application Level

If your target lesson task is a procedure, you will write a lesson objective at the application level that would require the learner to perform the procedure. For example, the lesson objective for the toothbrushing lesson would read: "You will be provided all needed equipment and have to brush your teeth following the steps provided in the lesson materials." For the credit task described above, the learning objective might read: "You will be given ten customer situations and write what deposit each customer must pay."

Avoid writing remember-level objectives for procedures. For example an objective that stated, "You will list the ten steps for brushing your teeth" would not be as effective as having the trainee actually do the procedure.

TRAINING PROCEDURES: INFORMATIONAL
INSTRUCTIONAL TECHNIQUES

When learning procedures, employees need two basic types of information:

1. a clear display of the steps that make up the procedure, with illustrations as appropriate
2. a follow-along demonstration.

It is a good idea for employees to have access to the steps in a written form as they participate in the demonstration. As you prepare to write up the procedural steps, take care to define them as discrete actions, especially for audiences unfamiliar with the task. Start each step with an action word. Break long, complicated procedures into several smaller procedures. As a rule of thumb, your procedures should not exceed 12 steps.

Formatting of Procedures in Manuals

Procedures are most cleanly presented in the training manual in *action* and *decision tables*. We'll look first at action tables and then at decision tables.

Figure 3–1 illustrates a procedure from the lesson on how to brush your teeth. The action table is divided into three columns:

FIGURE 3–1 Action Table with Separate Example Column

HOW TO BRUSH YOUR TEETH

Introduction   Now that you recognize the equipment you will need and we have discussed when you will need to brush your teeth, let's see how you brush.

Action Table   Here are the steps to follow to brush your teeth.

Step	Action	Example
1	Wet toothbrush with water from tap.	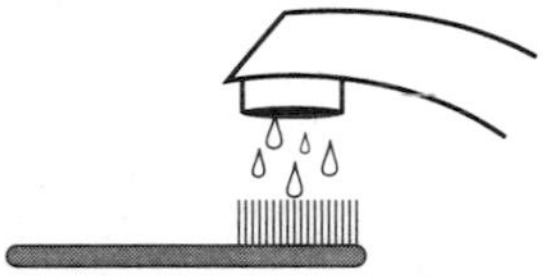
2	Apply about $\frac{1}{2}''$ of tooth paste on bristles.	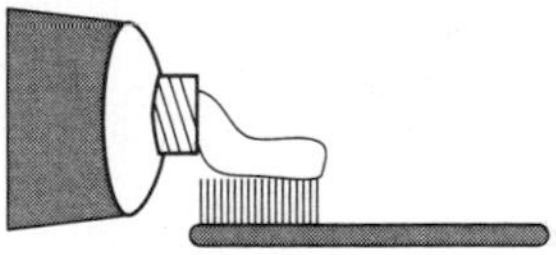
3	Hold handle of brush and move bristles up and down against teeth.	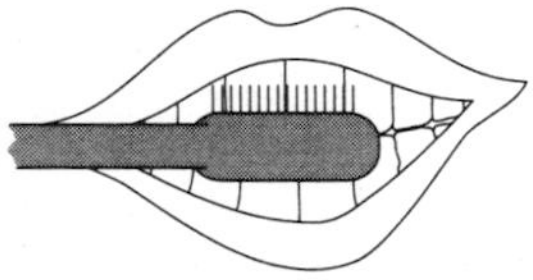
4	Open mouth and brush back teeth.	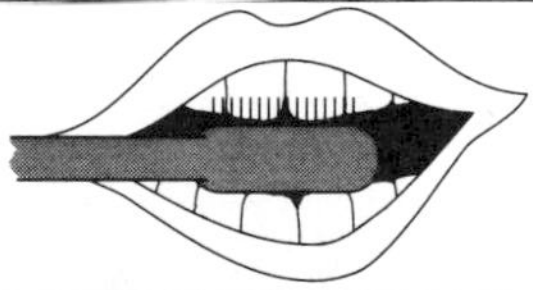
5	Use glass of water to rinse out mouth. Repeat twice.	
6	Wash off toothbrush and return equipment.	

Demonstration   Follow along as your instructor shows a videotape illustrating the steps to follow.

FIGURE 3–2 Action Table with Embedded Example

HOW TO PROCESS A WORK ORDER

Introduction   In the last unit, we discussed the importance of accurate accounting of company work orders. Now we will describe the procedure for processing a work order.

Action Table   This table describes how the District Accountant should process a work order

Step	Action
1.	Assign the work order a number from the Work Order Log Book
2.	File white copy in pending file by date
3.	Give pink copy to foreman
4.	When foreman returns copy, log in completion date in Work Order Log

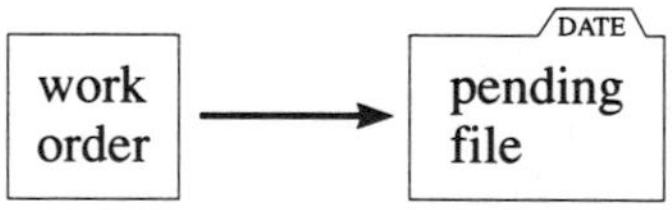

Step 1 — Work Order Log

Work Order Log		
Number	Start Date	Completion Date
236	6–18	8–24
237		

Assign Next Number

Step 2:

work order → pending file (DATE)

Step 4 — Work Order Log

Work Order Log		
Number	Start Date	Completion Date
236	6–18	8–24
237	6–30	

step, action, and *example.* Note that each step describes one simple, specific action. The newer the employee to the procedure, the smaller and more specific you need to make the steps. For example, new hires with little or no background in what you are teaching will require more detail than experienced employees who have some familiarity with the tasks.

Take a look at the entire page layout. A left-justified page heading that states, "How to . . ." tells the trainee about the content right away. A brief introduction at the top of the page that either relates the procedure to the rest of the lesson or explains its importance is also recommended. The Horn Structured Writing Guidelines recommend marginal labels and lines to separate sections. Figure 3–2 illustrates part of an action table for the procedure of processing work orders, in which the illustrations are embedded into the action steps. This method is recommended when not every step requires an illustration, since a third column would be empty part of the time. It is also easier to format a two-column table on the page.

Decision Tables

Branched procedures are best documented using decision tables. Figure 3–3 includes a decision table from the toothbrushing model lesson. Simple decision tables are written with a *If* . . . (condition statement) column followed by a *Then* . . . (action statement) column. They can be made a bit more complex, as in the "When to Brush" table, by adding the *And* . . . between the *If* . . . and *Then* . . . Figure 3–4 shows a decision table from a lesson on troubleshooting a computer display station. Be sure that you identify all the possible conditions under the *If* . . . column followed by appropriate action under *Then* . . . Note the overall page layout. The page heading should summarize the decision being made such as "When to Brush" or "How to Resolve Display Station Problems." The short introduction explains why the decision needs to be made, and marginal labels help the reader quickly identify relevant sections.

Combining Action and Decision Tables

As mentioned above, branched procedures include two or more linear procedures. Sometimes it is most efficient to embed the decision table in the action table, particularly when the decision is

FIGURE 3–3 Three-Column Decision Table

WHEN TO BRUSH

Guidelines   The following table describes situations when you should brush your teeth.

IF....	AND....	THEN....
You have just eaten	Your brush and paste are available	Brush your teeth
	Your brush and paste are NOT available	Rinse out mouth and brush later
You are going to bed	You have NOT brushed for four hours	Brush your teeth
	You have brushed in the last four hours	Wait until morning

relatively simple and directly tied into a larger action sequence. Figure 3–5 illustrates the first part of an action table. Step 5 embeds a short decision table into the overall action sequence.

Building the Demonstration into the Lesson Materials

In addition to the steps of the procedure, the instructor needs to provide the employee with a follow-along demonstration. To insure that the instructor does provide the demonstration, consider referencing it at the bottom of the action table with a short sentence labeled "Demonstration." The sentence will read "Your instructor will now provide a demonstration of how to . . . ." See the example at the bottom of Figure 3–1.

Formatting Procedures in Computer-Based Training

In Chapter 1, I stated that instructional methods determine instructional effectiveness, while the instructional media deliver the training. Trainees need the same information when learning procedures on the computer as in the classroom. They need clear statements of the steps involved in the procedure, as well as a follow-along demonstration.

FIGURE 3–4 Decision Table for Trouble Shooting

HOW TO RESOLVE DISPLAY STATION PROBLEMS

Introduction	Now that you recognize the display station's indicator lights, unit number, and profile, you are ready to learn the sequence of steps to be performed when checking these components.
Decision Table	Below is the sequence of questions to ask when troubleshooting a display station.

Step	Question
1	Is the STATUS SWITCH set to NORMAL?

If	Action
NO	Set to Normal
YES	Go to Step 2.

Step	Question
2	Are the READY, LINE SYNC and SYSTEM AVAILABLE lights ON?

If	Action
NO	Check POWER SWITCH, set to ON Check that station is plugged in. Check that outlet has power. Turn power switch off then on.
YES	Go to Step 3.

There are three differences to consider when designing CBT.

- First, since the computer lesson is usually intended to be self-instructional, it is even more critical to carefully include all required steps.

- Second, CBT requires a much shorter learning cycle than classroom instruction. The sequencing of information and practice must be very close to hold attention and support the internal processing of the information that results in learning. You should

FIGURE 3–5 **Decision Table Embedded in Action Table**

Step	Action
1.	• Complete PROGRAM INFORMATION FORM. • Forward completed form to CTRS Administrator.
2.	• Enter program information into computer. • Inform clerk(s) of assigned class numbers and julian dates.
3.	As 19-140s arrive for all programs... • Stamp 19-140s and fill in appropriate class number and julian date. • Enter participants' social security numbers into computer (NEW 19140). • As needed, enter changes to scheduled attendance of participants (NEW 19140).
4.	Monthly, run reports of participants scheduled to attend programs.
5.	Just prior to program start date... | If 19-140s...	Then
---	---
have been received prior to program	• enter participants' social security numbers into computer (TRAINING). • print computerized participant list. • forward list to consultant.
have *not* been received prior to program	• give consultant TEMPORARY PARTICIPANT LIST form.	

present a few steps at a time and have trainees follow along by trying out those steps in a simulation.

• Third, the screen imposes different format constraints than the 8 ½"-by-11" page.

When teaching trainees how to use on-line systems, you have two screen format choices: the *bottom-of-the-screen* or the *window format*. The choice depends primarily on the layout of the application screen. If you have room, compress the application screen upward and add instruction to the bottom of the instructional screen under a broken line or in a box as shown in Figure 3–6. If the parts of the application screen you want to teach are oriented toward the left- or right-hand side, you can place the instructional window on the inactive part of the screen as shown in Figure 3–7. Be sure to clearly identify the instructional section by placing instructional text in a box with space around it. Use a consistent, readable color for the instructional window which is different from the color of the application screen.

FIGURE 3–6 Instruction Placed at Bottom of Application Screen

```
CSNTRY - Unit A - Accounts Receivable                    See Job Aide  A-2
=========================================================================
*  *  *  *  *  *  *  *    ACCOUNTS RECEIVABLE SUB-MENU   *  *  *  *  *  *  *  *  *
       INQUIRY             .           SERVICE ORDER              ASSISTANCE
ABDI- BANK DEPOSITS INFO . ABCC- BALANCE CASH DRAWER . MENU- CIS MASTER MENU
APDI- PREPAID DEPOSIT     . ABDC- BANK DEPOSIT        .
APSI- PAYMENT SUMMARY     . ADTC- DEPOSIT TRANSACTION .
                          . AOCC- OPEN CASH DRAWER    .
                          . APAC- PAYMENTS            .
                          . ASMC- SUBLEDGER/MISC PYMT .
.  .  .  .  .  .  .    .  .  .  .  .  .  .  .    .  .  .  .  .    .  .  .  .
ENTER TRANSACTION CODE AND ACCOUNT IDENTIFIER      TRANSACTION CODE-
ACCOUNT NO-                  CUST NAME-                      METER -
SERVICE  NUMBER  FRCTN  PRFX  STREET NAME                    SUFX   APT  CITY
ADDRESS--
        o=====================================================o
        !   This is the ACCOUNTS RECEIVABLE SUB-MENU, AARA.   !
        !   The cash entry transaction codes you will use in  !
        !   in this course are highlighted.                   !
        o=====================================================o

=========================================================================
```

FIGURE 3–7 Instruction Placed in Window of Application Screen

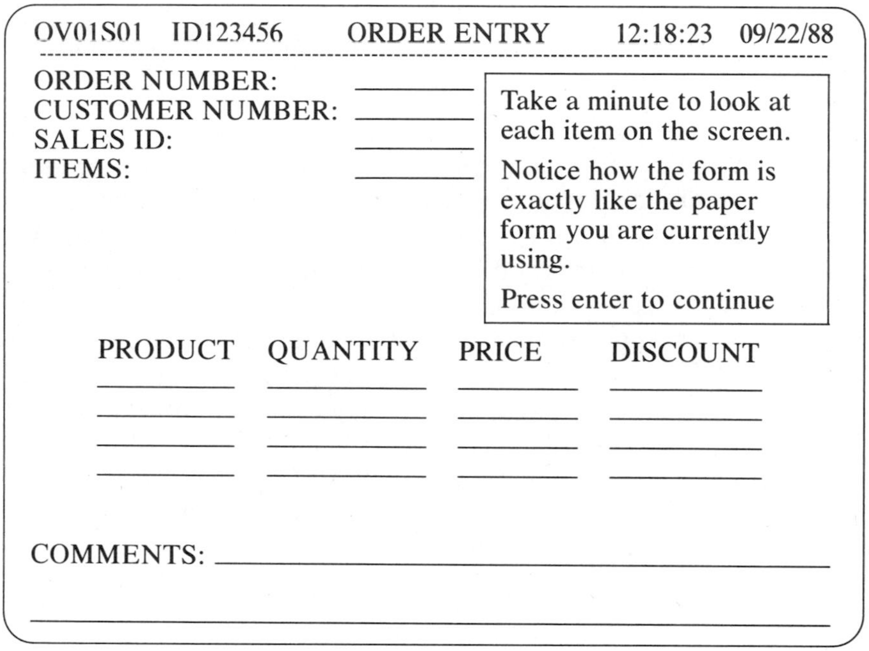

```
OV01S01   ID123456      ORDER ENTRY       12:18:23   09/22/88
---------------------------------------------------------------
ORDER NUMBER:         _____
CUSTOMER NUMBER:      _____    Take a minute to look at
SALES ID:             _____    each item on the screen.
ITEMS:                _____
                                  Notice how the form is
                                  exactly like the paper
                                  form you are currently
                                  using.

                                  Press enter to continue


     PRODUCT    QUANTITY    PRICE      DISCOUNT
     _____   _____   _____   _____
     _____   _____   _____   _____
     _____   _____   _____   _____
     _____   _____   _____   _____


COMMENTS: _____
_____
```

Teaching Non-Computer Procedures on Computer

The computer is an ideal delivery tool for training computer-related procedures. Remember that, to learn a procedure, the trainee must perform it. Unless the computer can simulate a task fairly faithfully, a different delivery medium should be considered for procedural training. If your computer system can display high-resolution graphics and has touch-screen capabilities, equipment simulations involving switches and dials can be developed to teach procedures of this type. Refer to some of the books cited on computer-based training for more information on these types of simulations. If your procedures involve more complex manipulation of equipment, your trainees should get hands-on practice on the equipment. Even in this case, you can use the computer to train information surrounding the procedure — such as equipment parts, interpretation of instrumentation, safety guidelines, and even a procedural overview — to be followed by hands-on laboratory work.

TRAINING PROCEDURES: INSTRUCTIONAL TECHNIQUES FOR PRACTICE

To be effective, training must provide relevant information interspersed with frequent practice exercises. Now that we have described the information displays that are best for teaching procedures, let's take a look at how to design practice that quickly gets the trainee doing the procedure.

Design of Practice for Classroom Use

Learning of procedures can be required at the remember or application level. Asking for remember performance where trainees memorize steps is generally a waste of time. Instead, give the step summaries in action or decision tables, and provide a follow-along demonstration. Then assign short exercises that require the trainee to perform the procedure. Figure 3–8 illustrates some practice exercises from the sample lessons described above that require the trainee to practice the procedure with the instructor's help. Encourage the trainees to follow along on the action or decision tables as they begin. With more practice, they will refer less and less to this memory support. It's a good idea, however, to let them keep a condensed version of the step summary that they can use while performing the task on the job until they are completely familiar with it.

FIGURE 3–8 Practice Exercises for Classroom Procedures

1. Linear Procedure
How to Brush Your Teeth
Now that you have seen a demonstration of the correct way to brush your teeth, use your action table and the material provided to brush your teeth. Your instructor will help you as needed.

2. Linear Procedure
How to Process a Work Order
You will be given sample work orders collected from the districts. Use the blank work order log and files to process each sample following the guidelines in your action table.

3. Branched Procedure
How to Resolve Display Station Problems
Analyze the indicator lights and unit number of the five display stations provided. Once you have determined the problem, fix it using your decision table as a guide.

Design of Practice for Computer-Based Training

It's important to have the trainee try out the steps provided in the training at almost the same time they see them. In fact, you can combine the information and practice portions of learning in CBT. You do this with a guided simulation in which you present a few steps and ask the trainee to fill out a portion of the application screen. Figure 3–9 shows a guided CBT simulation. After giving this step-by-step guided practice, you then provide more unstructured practice in an unguided simulation. This simulation often describes the data to be entered on paper rather than on the screen. This allows the trainee to work with the full application screen in a realistic simulation. An example of an unguided simulation appears in Figure 3–10.

EVALUATING LEARNING RESULTS

During the practice sessions help is provided to the trainees. Afterwards you need to evaluate how effectively they have mastered the procedure without help. The best way to do this for procedural learning is through a performance test. In the classroom the in-

FIGURE 3–9 Guided CBT Simulation

```
CSNTRY - Unit A - Accounts Receivable
================================================================================
*  *  *  *  *  *  *  *  *  OPEN CASH DRAWER  *  *  *  *  *  *  *  *  *
FILL IN APPLICABLE INFORMATION AND DEPRESS ENTER KEY
                                      OPER- HOH   DATE- 11/29     TIME- 08:00


         LOCATION- torino                BATCH NO- 5252

         EFFECTIVE DATE-   112998
  .  .  .  .  .  .  .  .  .  .  .  .  .  .  .  .  .  .  .  .  .  .  .
  o=====================================================================o
  :  Complete this service order with the following information:        :
  :     LOCATION - Your office location is TORINO local office,         :
  :     BATCH NO - You are authorized to use BATCH NUMBER 5252          :
  :     EFFECTIVE DATE - Today is NOVEMBER 29, 1998.                    :
  o=====================================================================o



================================================================================
```

FIGURE 3–10 Unguided CBT Simulation Using Data from Training Manual

Field:	Data:	Description:
1) EFF DATE	(use the effective date on the requisition)	
2) DOC #	159569	
3) name	tangen,andreas z	(format: comma between first & last; single space between first & initial)
4) STAT	NH	Status new hire
5) COMM	AD	Comment code, advertisement
6) EMP CAT	FR	Category full time regular

A. Training Manual

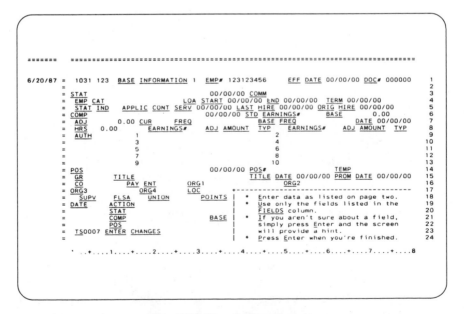

B. CBT Simulation Screen

Courtesy David Svoboda, Rockwell International, Administrative Services Center.

structor would use a checklist of steps similar to the procedure tables provided to the learners. The checklist would also include anticipated answers and scoring points such as the one illustrated in Figure 3–11. All trainees would be evaluated individually to determine that they could perform the procedure adequately.

If a number of instructors will be administering a performance test, instructor training on consistent use of the scoring guidelines should be provided. Gather all the instructors together and have them independently score the same performance. Check the scores for consistency. Discuss discrepancies. Repeat this process for several sessions until scores are consistent each time.

How stringently you evaluate trainee performance depends on the criticality of the procedure. If the job requires near-perfect performance from the start, you will require a high score on your performance test, which means you will have to invest more training time. Compare these two training environments. A major semiconductor manufacturer uses equipment that must be operated very carefully to avoid expensive product and equipment damage. They invest considerable training time and use a stringent performance test before letting the trainee operate the equipment. In contrast, a customer service department teaches operators how to process customer orders over the telephone. They require a less stringent level of proficiency than the semiconductor manufacturing plant before allowing trainees to take customer orders.

To evaluate performance on the computer, a simulation test similar to the simulation practice exercises can be developed which can be scored. Another approach would be to schedule an instructor-led follow-up class where questions could be asked and a performance test given to assess proficiency. A third option would be to require the trainee to produce some end-product, such as a budget spread sheet and transmit the result to a tutor.

PREVIEW OF CHAPTERS FOUR AND FIVE

By following the guidelines in this chapter, you will be able to efficiently train a major proportion of business/industrial tasks. There are always new terms and factual information to be learned with any procedure, and these should be included in the supporting section of your lesson. The next two chapters will describe how to teach two types of supporting information that accompany procedures: concepts and facts.

FIGURE 3–11 **Performance Test Checklist**

PDF Assessment

Directions:
- May use HELP or manual at any time
- May have PF key cheater card as a reference

Exercise	Answer	Points*
1. Log on to your System A ID.	(LOGON, or LOGONA, or GRAPH, ID, Password)	3
Q: What command is for logging on to System D?	(LOGOND or GRAPHD)	1
Q: What command is for logging on to System C?	(LOGONC)	1
2. Access the PDF main menu.	(PDF)	3
3. Use of PDF function to display the data sets under your ID.	(3.4, blank)	2
4. Return to the Utility Selection Menu.	(PF3/PF 15 twice or = 3)	2
5. Allocate a new sequential fixed block data set with:	(option 2, option A)	3
name 'ID.TRAIN.DATA' 5 tracks primary space 3 tracks secondary space record length — 250 bytes block size — 2500 bytes (on the default volume)		
Q: Why do we put zero for directory allocation?	(this is a sequential data set; there is no directory)	2
6. Rename the above data set to 'ID.TRAINING.DATA'	(option R)	1
7. Delete this data set.	(option D)	1
Q: How do you know the delete worked?	(message in upper right-hand corner)	2

*Based on Importance

The Content-Performance Matrix: Concepts

	Facts	Concepts	Processes	Procedures	Principles
Apply	/////	Classify new Examples *Which file name is valid?* *A. 043MYFILE* *B. MYFILE9*		Perform the Procedure *Log onto the Computer*	
Remember		Remember the Definition *Define Valid File Name*		Remember the Steps *List the Steps to Log onto the Computer*	

CHAPTER 4

How to Teach Concepts

CHAPTER SUMMARY

- A concept is a class of items that share common features and are known by a common name. All concept groups include multiple specific examples. Most technical training involves many concepts associated with the procedures employees need to learn for effective job performance.

- Concepts are made up of critical features that all concepts of a class share in common, and irrelevant features on which specific examples of the concept vary.

- Concepts with parts and boundaries are concrete concepts, while less tangible concepts that cannot be illustrated with a diagram are abstract Concepts.

- Concepts can be learned at the remember level by memorization of the critical features or definition of the concept. Memorization of definitions is not recommended. At the application level, learners can discriminate target concepts from other concepts.

- Information displays for teaching concepts include definitions, examples, non-examples, and analogies. Examples for concrete concepts take the form of diagrams, while those for abstract concepts will need to be presented verbally. Initial examples should reflect typical instances that systematically vary one feature at a time while later examples call on less common instances.

• Information displays can be formatted for training manuals by using marginal labels for definitions, examples, non-examples, and analogies. For computer-based-training, screen overlays or builds can use a variety of formats to gradually display the same informational types. It is important to maintain uncluttered screens and present reasonably small amounts of information at one time.

• Practice in both classroom and CBT should encourage accurate discrimination through classification practice — asking trainees to correctly identify the new concepts from a group of valid and invalid examples. This can be done using real examples or by paper-and-pencil exercises. On computer, common formats for classification practice include Yes-No, multiple choice, matching, and multiple discrimination.

• To evaluate concept learning, format test questions like the practice exercises but use new examples. Ask trainees to identify the target concept from a group of related concepts.

In Chapter 3, I described how to train basic business/industrial procedures. While training procedures you will usually make reference to equipment, tools, etc., using technical terms involved in the steps you are training. Technical specialists often omit this supporting information because it is so familiar to them they forget it is new to their learners. For example, suppose Step 5 in your procedure is: "Place the zygometer in the reactive receptacle of the erylitizer when it reaches the suctorial stage." If you were teaching this procedure and never explained zygometers, reactive receptacles, erylitizers or suctorial stages, your trainees would be unable to do the procedure. Not because the procedure is difficult or has not been effectively taught, but because the supporting information has been left out. As a result the trainees may feel stupid or frustrated. That's why it's so important for you to systematically identify and teach all supporting information.

In this chapter I will describe how to train one type of associated information: concepts. After defining concepts and showing some

FIGURE 4–1 When supporting information is left out, trainees are confused.

examples, I'll describe how concepts are learned at the remember and application levels. I will draw on the considerable instructional research on ways of teaching concepts effectively. Informational formats for teaching concepts will be illustrated for both the training manual and computer. These will be followed by guidelines and examples for the design of practice exercises. As with all types of content (except facts), I will emphasize teaching at the application rather than the remember level. Finally, I will discuss how to determine that your students have successfully acquired the concepts at the application level.

WHAT IS A CONCEPT?

Our everyday language includes many concepts, such as chair, mammal, house, woman. A concept is a mental representation or prototype of objects or ideas for which multiple specific examples exist. All of the concepts above represent a general class of "things," containing many real instances. The ability to represent reality in concepts makes our language and mental representations very efficient. Suppose you had to hold a separate mental representation for every chair or house. Your memory would be cluttered by information that would take up resources more productively devoted to processing information.

Concepts all have *critical features,* or characteristics, and *irrelevant features*. The critical features are always associated with the particular concept; the irrelevant features vary from specific example to example. Consider the concept "chair." All chairs share about four critical features. Nearly all chairs are intended for a single sitter and have a seat, a back, and some support from the floor to the seat. What are some of the irrelevant, or varying, features of chairs? Color, presence of arms, and type of support from the floor (typically legs but occasionally a podium, a rocker, or wheels) are just a few. As illustrated in Figure 4–2, your mental representation of "chair" has abstracted the critical features, allowing you to recognize many examples of chairs which vary on the irrelevant features. Even if you were to see a type of chair unfamiliar to you, in a foreign country, for example, you would probably recognize it as a chair, based on the core features you hold in your mental representation. This is what makes concepts much more efficient than facts, which, as we will see in the next chapter, must be individually held in memory.

Types of Concepts

It will be helpful in the next section on teaching of concepts to distinguish between two basic classes of concepts: concrete and abstract. Concrete concepts have defined parts and boundaries that

FIGURE 4–2 Concepts share critical features and vary on irrelevant features.

you can draw and label. "Bicycle," "house," and "chair" are examples. Abstract concepts are less tangible and cannot be directly represented using diagrams. Examples of abstract concepts include "integrity," "credit," "deposit," and "goal."

Identifying Your Technical Concepts

One of your major challenges as a technical expert will be to identify the concepts in your technical area that must be included in your training. It's a challenge because you are so familiar with most of them that you will tend to forget that your learners are not. A good way to identify your concepts is to examine the steps you have documented in your procedure. Be alert for any terminology unfamiliar to your learners that would qualify as a concept. For example, suppose the toothbrushing procedure illustrated in Figure 3–1 on page 45 was for an alien learner. In talking to the alien, the instructor in Figure 4–3 discovers it is familiar with mouths, teeth, and water. Therefore there are two major concepts it doesn't know related to the procedure to be trained: toothbrush and toothpaste.

One good way to identify your technical concepts is to refer to the procedural steps you have listed in your action or decision tables. Each new concept in the procedure will need to be separately

FIGURE 4–3 **Interview the learning audience to determine what related information they need.**

trained in your lesson. Before I describe how to train concepts, let's take a look at how concepts are processed psychologically at the remember and application levels of learning.

CHECK YOUR UNDERSTANDING

To be sure you can identify concepts, try the short exercise on page 241.

LEARNING CONCEPTS AT REMEMBER
AND APPLICATION LEVELS

Recall that all of the content types except facts can be psychologically processed at a remember and at an application level. At the remember level, the employee can recall the major critical features of the concept. For example, she might say: "A chair is a type of furniture intended for one sitter that has a seat, back, and support from the floor." Basically she is giving a definition which is a summary of the critical features of the concept. However, as we see in Figure 4–4, just because a learner can state a definition does not

FIGURE 4–4 Being able to remember the features of a concept does not mean the learner will be able to recognize it.

mean that she could actually recognize the concept when she saw it. The real reason for teaching concepts in business and industry is to help employees identify the tools or technical terms they will be using in their jobs. That psychological skill is called discrimination — the ability to distinguish the concept from others. In everyday terms we would say, "Do they know one when they see one?" This skill will result from learning to process concepts at the application level.

At the application level, the employee can identify or discriminate the concept by picking a valid example from a number of similar items. For example, you might give your learner a picture of ten items of furniture and ask them to circle all the chairs. This shows they have assimilated the critical features successfully so they can identify specific instances of the concept. If one of your action steps were to place the zygometer on the reactive receptacle of the erylitizer during the suctorial stage, the employee would need to be able to identify zygometers, erylitizers, reactive receptacles, and suctorial stages from the many other concepts in the work environment.

Writing Concept Learning Objectives at the Application Level

If the supporting or "hidden mental skills" section of your lesson includes a few critical concepts or several less critical concepts, you will need to write a supporting learning objective to establish a learning goal for this section. Typically, concept learning objectives are secondary to the major objective in a procedural lesson. For example, note the two lesson objectives written on the toothbrush lesson introductory page in Figure 2–2 on page 26. The major is that the learner will brush his teeth correctly — a procedure. But the secondary objective asks the learner to identify toothbrush and toothpaste — two concepts.

Write your concept objective at the application level by using an action verb that involves a classification activity. In the toothbrush lesson the learner will be given typical bathroom supplies and asked to pick out the target concepts — the toothbrush and toothpaste — from the rest. Here the trainee is classifying the target concepts by picking them out. Let's take a look now at how to efficiently teach concepts so that employees will achieve the learning objective of making the critical concept discriminations.

TRAINING CONCEPTS: INFORMATIONAL
INSTRUCTIONAL TECHNIQUES

Instructional methods include giving required information in formatted displays and providing relevant practice exercises with feedback. To evaluate your success you need to test to be sure your objectives have been achieved. In this section, I'll first discuss the information requirements for teaching concepts, and illustrate how your would format this information in a workbook and on computer. Then I'll describe how to design practice to support application-level learning, as well as how to test for acquisition.

Years of instructional research have identified the critical information required to successfully teach concepts. When teaching concepts you must always provide a *definition* and *examples* of the concept. If possible, you can also provide *non-examples* and *analogies*. Let's look at each of these.

The Definition   A definition is a statement of the critical features associated with a concept. Writing a good definition may be more difficult than you realize, especially if you are so familiar with the concept that you need to really think about the key features. Our definition for chair might be: "A type of furniture intended for a single sitter which includes a seat, back, and floor support." Or suppose you were teaching the concept *nerd*. The definition might read: "A male student type who is somewhat socially awkward and typically can be identified by a calculator and/ or writing device in the front breast pocket, high-water pants, white socks, cowlick, and skinny body type."

The Examples   An example is a real instance of the concept. Once you have presented the definition, you make it concrete by presenting examples. If the concept is very simple, a couple of examples might suffice. However if the concept is complex, with many features, you will want to provide several examples, each of which contains all the critical features and in which *irrelevant features are systematically varied one at a time*. As a general rule you want to start off with a typical example and move to less common illustrations.

Suppose you were teaching the concrete concept "dog" to a young child. After a general definition, you first show a picture of

FIGURE 4-5 Seeing varied examples allows the learner to abstract a mental prototype of the concept.

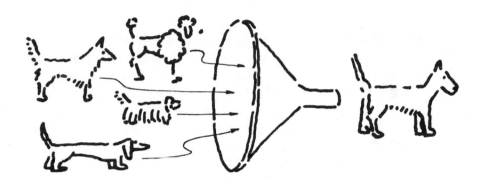

a "typical" dog. You might decide on a German shepherd. Your next example should vary only one or two of the irrelevant features. You might use a collie, where you have varied hair length and color. Your next example might be a dachshund, where you have varied size and body proportion. You might also include a poodle and perhaps a couple of more exotic varieties. Carefully choosing a range of examples is critical. As illustrated in Figure 4–5, the learner looks at these examples, and abstracts the critical features from the irrelevant ones. The child would unconsciously be noting that dogs can have long, short, or curly hair; can have various colors, sizes, and body shape; but that all of them have the critical canine features, such as a muzzle, tail, etc.

Examples of graphic concepts such as "dog" and "erylitizer" should be presented in the form of illustrations. If the concept has specific parts that are relevant, use a key-pointed diagram to illustrate the concept such as that used in the Nerd lesson in Figure 4–10. Often, however, your concepts will be abstract, and you will need to construct examples in verbal formats. For example, if you are teaching the concept of good credit, an example might be: "Mrs. Jones has applied for service from our company. In checking her prior payment records, we find that she is recently divorced and did not have service in her name. But we discover she owns her own home and so can qualify for a good credit rating." As a technical specialist, you can save lesson development time by collecting a number of examples from the work environment and modifying them to meet your instructional needs.

   The Non-examples   When teaching concepts a definition and examples are essential. It is also helpful to present non-examples and analogies. A Non-example is an instance of a closely related concept which could be confused with the lesson concept. Therefore you should use non-examples in situations where concept A is often confused with concept B. After showing several examples, show the non-example and explain why it is not an instance of the concept.

   Note the instructor in Figure 4–6 using a chair as a non-example of a dog. Would this be an effective non-example to use? Probably not, because, other than the four legs, the two concepts share no common features. A better non-example would be a concept whose features overlap those of the dog sufficiently to be potentially confusing. A cat is one obvious choice.

   Think of the function of a non-example in terms of the Venn diagram illustrated in Figure 4–7. Note that the non-example B overlaps some of the features of the valid concept A and so can be confused. The effective non-example stresses the ways the two concepts are distinct to minimize confusion.

FIGURE 4–6 Choose appropriate non-examples to illustrate the concept.

FIGURE 4–7 Using Non-examples to Teach Concepts

OVERLAPPING
FEATURES

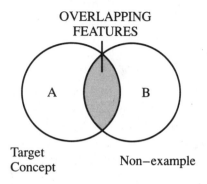

Target
Concept

Non–example

FIGURE 4–6 Choose appropriate non-examples to illustrate the concept.

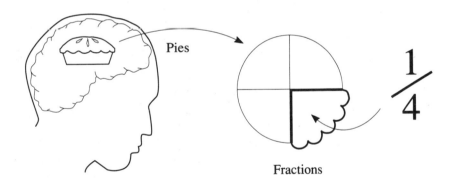

Analogies An analogy is a representation which corresponds with a concept in function or form but which is otherwise dissimilar. Analogies are typically drawn from a domain different from that of the material being trained. A classic example of using an analogy to teach a concept is the pie analogy used to teach the concept of fraction. The teacher typically shows how the pie can be cut into halves and then into quarters, and so on. Analogies are efficient instructional techniques because they allow you to relate an unfamiliar concept to something the learner already knows, usually in a totally different domain of knowledge. While analogies are very powerful instructional tools, it is often difficult to think of an analogy that fits the concept you are teaching. The key to an effective analogy is to find something familiar to your learners that shares critical characteristics with your concept. Again you need to know about the background knowledge of your target audience. A technical analogy that works well for an engineering target audience might be meaningless for a less specialized population. If your target-audience background is very broad, you will need to rely on everyday analogies that will be relevant to all. Analogies can be presented in either pictures or verbal formats. Whenever possible use pictures, as they are much more memorable than verbal descriptions.

I have presented the basic informational types needed to teach concepts i.e. definitions and examples, and, when possible, non-examples and analogies. Now let's take a look at how you might format this information, first in a training manual and then on computer.

Formatting of Concepts in Manuals

For manuals the structured writing style introduced in Chapter 2 is recommended. To introduce concepts, use a left-justified heading "What is Concept X?" Then use marginal labels of "definition," "example," "non-example" and "analogy" next to those elements of the lesson. Each section would be separated from the others by a solid line. Or you could embed the labels in the text and separate the sections with white space. Your objective is to provide visible headings and to separate distinct bodies of information. Figure 4–9 illustrates these format guidelines for the concrete concept of "toothbrush." The left-justified heading "What is a Toothbrush?" identifies the concept lesson. Note the marginal labels and the example and non-example which, since toothbrush is a graphic concept, are presented as diagrams.

For another example, take a look at the Nerd lesson in Figure 4–10. An introduction sets the context for the lesson. The definition is made especially clear by the use of bullets to emphasize the critical features. In this lesson the graphic example is reinforced by some famous examples, non-examples, and an analogy. The graphic example uses a key-pointed table to reinforce the critical characteristics.

FIGURE 4–9 Information Displays for Concept Lesson on Toothbrush

HOW TO BRUSH YOUR TEETH

Introduction   Proper cleaning of teeth is essential to maintaining them in usable condition. This lesson will provide the procedure for good maintenance of teeth.

Equipment   To brush your teeth you will need
Needed
                 • a toothbrush, and

                 • toothpaste.

WHAT IS A TOOTHBRUSH?

Definition   A *toothbrush* is a small brush with a long handle, usually made out of plastic, used exclusively for the purpose of brushing teeth.

Example

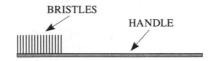

Non-example

                 A hair brush is much larger and has a shorter handle. It would not fit in your mouth.

Ownership   For sanitary reasons, every individual owns and uses only his or her own toothbrush.

FIGURE 4–10 Information Displays for Concept Lesson on Nerds

IDENTIFICATION OF COMMON STUDENT TYPES
Lesson 3 — The Nerd

Introduction	So far in this course you have learned to identify two common student types, the Campus Queen and the B.M.O.C. You will now learn to identify the Nerd, perhaps the most complex and difficult student type to understand. In this lesson only the male species will be considered.
Definition	A *Nerd* is a male student type that can be identified by the following characteristics: • A calculating and/or writing device prominently displayed in the front breast pocket • High-water pants • Cowlick • White socks • Weighs 98 lbs. or less
Famous Examples	• Pee Wee • Woody Allen • Charlie Brown
Famous Non-examples	• John Wayne — not a Nerd because he doesn't carry a calculating device • Superman — not a Nerd because he doesn't wear white socks • Telly Savalas — not a Nerd because he has no cowlick • Steve Garvey — not a Nerd because his pants are never high-water
An Analogy	In a sense, a Nerd is similar to a Volkswagen. Like a Volkswagen, the Nerd is slight of build, unassuming in appearance, and quite easily distinguished from more sophisticated models.
Graphic Display	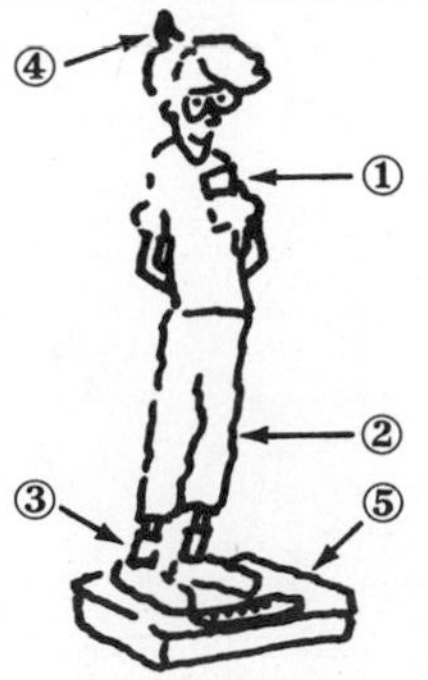 *Characteristics of Nerd* ① Calculating and/or writing device ② High-water pants ③ White socks ④ Cowlick ⑤ 98 lbs. or less

FIGURE 4–11 Information Displays from Concept Lesson on Payment Record

---

WHAT IS A GOOD PAYMENT RECORD?

Introduction   One criterion for establishing customer credit is to verify a good payment record for customers who have had service with our Company for a year or more. In this lesson you will learn how to determine if a customer has a good payment record.

Definition   A good payment record refers to a payment history of a year or more where no more than one warning notice was sent for an overdue bill.

Example   Mrs. Marks has had service with our Company since October of 1986. Her payment history appears below. Note she has had only one warning notice. Her payment history is good.

PAYMENT HISTORY SUMMARY SCREEN

MRS. GALE MARKS

JANUARY	PIF	JULY	PP
FEBRUARY	PP	AUGUST	PIF
•• MARCH	W	SEPTEMBER	PIF
APRIL	PIF	OCTOBER	PIF
MAY	PIF	NOVEMBER	PP
JUNE	—	DECEMBER	—

Non-example   Mr. Jones says he has had service for more than five years. His payment history appears below. Since he has had two warning notices, he does not have a good payment record.

PAYMENT HISTORY SUMMARY SCREEN

MR. RALPH JONES

JANUARY	PIF	JULY	PP
FEBRUARY	PP	•• AUGUST	W
•• MARCH	W	SEPTEMBER	PIF
APRIL	PIF	OCTOBER	PIF
MAY	PIF	NOVEMBER	PP
JUNE	—	DECEMBER	—

FIGURE 4–12 Information Displays from Training Registration Lesson

---

WHAT IS A VALID TRAINING ACTIVITY NUMBER

Definition	A valid training activity number is a seven-digit number consisting of: • 2 or 3 alphabetic characters that classify the training • 3 or 4 numeric characters identifying the course

---

Valid
Codes

The valid training classifications are:

Code	Classification
CBT	Computer Based Training
QTL	Classroom Instruction
QC	Office Computing
QTS	Self Study
HRD	Human Resource Development
IBM	IBM External
OUT	All other external courses

Valid
Examples

OUT0048
CBT0025
HRD001
QC341

Non-examples   OUR5469
0002IBM
QTSABC58R
HRD50

Finally, let's take a look at several examples from actual business training manuals. Figure 4–11 is from a Customer Service training manual developed for a major utility. The lesson is on how to establish customer credit. This page teaches the concept of "a good payment record." Figure 4–12 is from a lesson on how to use an automated training registration and record-keeping system. One of the concepts involved in using the system is the "training activity number." Note that, in this situation, it is the non-examples — wrong alphabetic code, reversed alphabetic and numeric characters, too many characters, and not enough characters — that are systematically varied. This careful selection of a range of non-examples helps reinforce the critical characteristics of the valid training activity number.

A third lesson example illustrates an efficient way to teach two related concepts simultaneously. Figure 4–13 teaches the difference between defects and defectives for a quality control lesson. Note that the definitions and examples are placed in a table. The examples for one concept serve as non-examples for the other. The visual provides a graphic illustration that effectively depicts the differences in the two concepts.

Now that we have seen a number of ways that the definitions, examples, non-examples, and analogies can be formatted in a training manual, let's see how you would display similar information on a screen in CBT.

Formatting Concept Information in Computer-Based Training

The informational displays needed to teach concepts are the same regardless of the media used. We are still working with definitions, examples, non-examples, and analogies. The major difference is the layout on the 80-line-by-24-column screen. There are several alternative screen formats to use, depending on the length of your definition, the number of features involved in the concepts, and the number of examples and non-examples. One important principle in CBT is to avoid screens crowded with new information all at once, especially for novice learners. You can add short chunks of information to a complex screen a bit at a time using a technique called overlaying, or screen-building. Figure 4–14 illustrates presentation of the abstract concept "learning objective." Note that the critical features of the objective are overlaid on the left-hand side of the screen with an example on the right. Once all features are presented, a complete example is shown by combining all the parts.

FIGURE 4–13 Information Displays for Teaching Two Related Concepts

---

DEFECTS vs. DEFECTIVES

Introduction As you can see in column 4 of the Job Aid, we are at the next decision point in determining which control chart to use. Remember that this concept is used for attribute data only.

Look at the definitions and examples provided below. Then turn to the next page for some practice with sampling and defect concepts.

Definitions

	DEFINITION	EXAMPLES
DEFECTS	• Number of faults per 1 item Fault(s) which cause an item to fail to meet specification requirements. There can be more than one defect per given part	• 3 typing errors on a page • 15 holes on a roll of paper • Water tank with 10 leaks
DEFECTIVES	• Number of items with 1 or more faults	• 1 defective page • 3 defective rolls • 5 defective water tanks

LEAKING WATER TANKS

Defects Equals 5

Defectives Equals 3

FIGURE 4–14 CBT Information Screens for Concept Lesson

Instructional Objectives	1 of 10

Instructional objectives have 3 parts:

- An action   Will isolate the fault
  statement

Instructional Objectives	2 of 10

Instructional objectives have 3 parts:

- An action   Will isolate the fault
  statement
- A condition   Given schematic and
  statement   diagnostics

Instructional Objectives	3 of 10

Instructional objectives have 3 parts:

- An action   Will isolate the fault
  statement
- A condition   Given schematic and
  statement   diagnostics
- A criterion   With 100% accuracy

Instructional Objectives	4 of 10

Putting them all together:

Condition + Action + Criterion

Given schematic diagram and diagnostics, the learner will isolate the fault with 100% accuracy.

Figure 4–15 illustrates introductory screens from a database software course developed for new computer users. Effective use of a common office analogy is used to present the concepts of database and file. The characteristics of a valid file name are overlaid individually with supporting examples and non-examples in boxes below the definition. There are a variety of formats one can use to display the information on computer screens. The main point is to include the critical information and to present it in clean, uncluttered displays.

Once you have presented the major characteristics with examples and non-examples, you will need to provide practice to insure psychological processing of the information you have just given. Let's take a look at how to design practice exercises that accomplish your goal.

TRAINING CONCEPTS: INSTRUCTIONAL
TECHNIQUES FOR PRACTICE

Recall from above that your major purpose is to get employees to discriminate concepts so they can identify them during job performance. For example, when working with zygometers, it's not as

FIGURE 4–15 CBT Information Screens for Concept Lesson

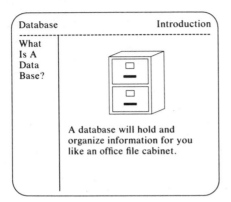

Database   Introduction

What
Is A
Data
Base?

A database will hold and organize information for you like an office file cabinet.

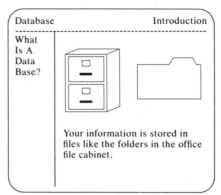

Database   Introduction

What
Is A
Data
Base?

Your information is stored in files like the folders in the office file cabinet.

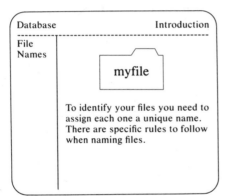

Database   Introduction

File
Names

myfile

To identify your files you need to assign each one a unique name. There are specific rules to follow when naming files.

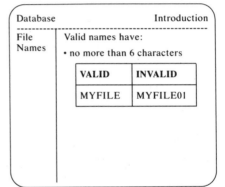

Database   Introduction

File
Names

Valid names have:

• no more than 6 characters

VALID	INVALID
MYFILE	MYFILE01

Database   Introduction

File
Names

Valid file names have:

• no more than 6 characters

• leading alpha character

VALID	INVALID
MYFILE	MYFILE01
MYFILE	12MYFILE

Database   Introduction

File
Names

Valid file names have:

• no more than 6 characters

• leading alpha character

• alphanumerics only

VALID	INVALID
MYFILE	MYFILE01
MYFILE	12MYFILE
MYFIL2	MYFIL&

important that trainees can define a zygometer as it is that they know one when they see it — a skill called discrimination. Therefore, you will want to design practice to match your learning objective at the application level of performance.

To design practice at the application level, give the learner an assortment of new examples and non-examples that were not used in the lesson, and ask him to identify the valid examples. In our dog lesson for a child, we might present a page of animal pictures, asking the child to circle all the dogs. This is referred to as classification practice, because the trainee classifies each sample as a valid or invalid example of the concept. Successful classification indicates that the employee can discriminate effectively. This type of practice can be designed for both classroom and computer training.

Design of Practice for Classroom Use

In the classroom you can use a variety of paper-and-pencil formats or performance-type classification exercises. A performance exercise presents real objects that are classified by the learner. A common industrial example involves practice used when training inspectors. New inspectors must learn to discriminate between defective and nondefective parts. A performance exercise gives them ten parts to sort into reject and accept piles. A practice session on the concepts "toothbrush" and "toothpaste" might ask the trainee to pick out the brush and toothpaste from an assortment of common bathroom articles. If it is impractical to provide real objects, or the concept is more abstract, use paper-and-pencil exercises.

Figure 4–16 illustrates the classification exercise designed to teach customer service representatives how to identify a good payment record. For each customer example provided, the learner is asked to indicate the credit status, i.e. good or poor, and to state the reason. Having them state the reason eliminates the lucky-guess syndrome and helps the instructor verify the student's understanding. The exercise that goes with the concept lesson presented in Figure 4–12 is shown in Figure 4–17. Paper-and-pencil practice can ask the trainee to circle the correct instances or it can use a matching or multiple-choice format. The main point is to design the practice to get learners to classify the concept correctly to show that they know one when they see one.

FIGURE 4–16 Classification Exercise for Customer Service Lesson

PRACTICE:
For each credit record, determine whether the credit status is good or poor. Give the reason for your answer.

1.

PAYMENT HISTORY SUMMARY SCREEN

MS. MARGARET JONES

JANUARY	PIF	** JULY	W
FEBRUARY	PP	AUGUST	PIF
MARCH	W	SEPTEMBER	PIF
** APRIL	PIF	OCTOBER	
MAY	PIF	NOVEMBER	
JUNE	—	DECEMBER	

Credit Status:

Reason:

2.

PAYMENT HISTORY SUMMARY SCREEN

MR. MARK HOMES

JANUARY	PIF	** JULY	W
FEBRUARY	PP	AUGUST	PIF
MARCH	PIF	SEPTEMBER	PIF
APRIL	PIF	OCTOBER	
MAY	PIF	NOVEMBER	
JUNE	—	DECEMBER	

Credit Status:

Reason:

3.

PAYMENT HISTORY SUMMARY SCREEN

MS. GLENDA ROBERTS

JANUARY	PIF	** JULY	W
FEBRUARY	PP	AUGUST	PIF
MARCH	PIF	SEPTEMBER	PIF
APRIL	PIF	OCTOBER	
MAY	PIF	NOVEMBER	
JUNE	—	DECEMBER	

Credit Status:

Reason:

FIGURE 4–17 **Classification Exercise for Training Activity Number Lesson**

For each training activity number below, indicate whether it is valid or invalid. For invalid numbers, correct them to make them valid:

1. HRD02
2. RQS0345
3. CBT0455
4. 0048CBT
5. HRD4967
6. IBM7*6

It is often efficient to combine several related concepts in a classification exercise. The practice exercise illustrated in Figure 4–18 asks the trainee to distinguish between defects and defectives as well as another concept pair — constant and varying sample size. The opportunity to distinguish both concept pairs simultaneously is provided in this exercise.

Design of Practice for Computer-Based Training

Your strategy to get learners to discriminate newly learned concepts correctly should be the same on CBT as in the classroom exercises, i.e. give them samples of the concept (along with invalid samples) to identify. In CBT, however, the structure of the practice is constrained a bit by the need to judge responses, all of which must be anticipated and built into the program. Most systems cannot handle extensive free-form answers such as the classroom exercise in Figure 4–16 where learners stated why a given credit example was good or poor. However, the same learning can result from a more structured format.

To provide classification practice CBT can readily handle multiple-choice, matching, multiple discrimination, or dichotomous responses (e.g. "Yes/No" or "T/F"). Using the lesson on instructional objectives as an example, the CBT author has created a multiple-choice format illustrated in Figure 4–19, where the trainee must identify the learning objective that best fits the criteria. By contrast, Figure 4–20 includes two different formats for

FIGURE 4–18 **Practice on Multiple Concepts**

PRACTICE:
Instructions: Read the following statements and determine
whether you used
    a.   constant or varying sampling
    b.   defect or defective data

Underline your responses and explain your reasons
for your choices.

1. You were asked to inspect the condition of fifty carpet bolts.
   You decide to inspect one square foot on each bolt and tally
   the number of samples with either stains or holes.

   a.   constant or varying sample size _____

   b.   defects or defective data _____

2. Sam requested information regarding the quality of the
   machine part #16-33B. He received an itemized report that
   showed the different sample sizes inspected and the number of
   defects each sample had.

Sample Lot	# of Defects
A: 2	4
B: 10	5
C: 25	2
D: 2	8

   a.   constant or varying sample size _____

   b.   defects or defective data _____

3. Fred needs information about ¾" bolts for an annual
   production meeting. He decides to sample fifteen bolts within
   the first hour of production, thirty-five bolts within the fourth
   hour of production, and three bolts within the last hour of
   production. For each sample he tallies information about each
   bolt that has one or more flaws.

   a.   constant or varying sample size _____

   b.   defects or defective data _____

FIGURE 4–19 Classification Exercise in CBT Lesson on Learning Objectives

Instructional Objectives   Practice 3

Type in the letter of the best instructional objective:

a.   Given three credit summaries, you will circle all that meet
     credit criteria

b.   You will know how to apply credit criteria to customer credit
     summaries

c.   Given three credit summaries, you will mark all that meet
     credit criteria with 100% accuracy

>   _____

FIGURE 4–20 Two CBT Formats for Classification Exercise on Valid File Names

Database   Practice 2

Is this a valid file name?
Type in Yes or No:
_____   3RDFIL

Database   Practice 3

Type an X next to each valid file name:
_____   3RDFILE
_____   FILE03
_____   FILE-3

Dichotomous Format   Multiple Discrimination Format

achieving classification practice on CBT in the lesson on valid file names. One version uses a Yes/No format. A screen-build can present questions individually, but by keeping each completed question on the screen the trainee benefits from reviewing all of them as he progresses. Alternatively, a multiple discrimination screen asks the learner to identify valid examples from a number of sample file names. This would be a good review question, since it is more comprehensive and thus more difficult than the Yes/No format that gives the trainee feedback one example at a time. After completion of the lesson either in classroom or computer training, you will want to verify that the learner can successfully discriminate the new concepts.

Evaluating Learning Results

Whether your training takes place in the classroom or on CBT you will want to be sure that your learning objective has been achieved. Can the learner successfully discriminate the new concept? If she can't you will want to arrange for additional practice and assistance. To verify that concepts have been successfully acquired you should create a test to match your learning objective, similar in format to the practice exercises shown above. If your objective stated that trainees would identify the toothbrush and toothpaste from a variety of bathroom supplies, both the practice and the test would provide supplies and ask learners to pick out the toothbrush and toothpaste. Your test items should use different examples from those used during practice sessions. No help would be provided during the testing situation. On CBT you can track the answers and provide additional help for material not learned adequately by automatically branching the trainee to review and practice sections (which should be different from the original lesson), or by providing advisement such as that shown in Figure 4–21.

FIGURE 4–21 CBT Advisement Based on Test Results

CUSTOMER CREDIT ESTABLISHMENT   UNIT 3

You scored a total of 86% overall on this unit. Most of the mistakes you made relate to establishment of commercial customer credit accounts.

You might want to review the procedures applicable to commercial accounts in Manual 3–2 and work through extra practice CBT Exercise 3–5.

PREVIEW OF CHAPTER FIVE

When you are teaching technical procedures and principles, there is always supporting information that your trainees will need, in order to understand the steps or guidelines of the major lesson task. Most of this supporting information is in the form of either concepts or facts. By following the guidelines in this chapter you will be able to identify and train the concepts in your technical area. Chapter Five will teach you to identify and instruct the supporting factual information your trainees will need.

The Content-Performance Matrix: Facts

	Facts	Concepts	Processes	Procedures	Principles
Apply	(shaded)	Classify new Examples *Which file name is valid?* *A. 043MYFILE* *B. MYFILE9*		Perform the Procedure *Log onto the Computer*	
Remember	**Remember the Facts** *What is your computer password?*	Remember the Definition *Define Valid File Name*		Remember the Steps *List the Steps to Log onto the Computer*	

CHAPTER 5

How to Teach Factual Information

CHAPTER SUMMARY

- Factual information consists of either one-of-a-kind associations among concepts or individual specific items, each example of which is identical.

- The individual specific items are generally concrete in nature, with parts and boundaries, while the associations among concepts are expressed as fact statements.

- When listing the steps that make up your procedures, look at each step to identify all concepts and facts associated with the procedure.

- Facts can be processed at the remember level only. This means they are not transformed psychologically but held "as is" in memory. Because storage and retrieval of information from human memory can be inefficient, memorization of factual information is to be avoided when possible. It is recommended that you avoid writing learning objectives that ask trainees to recall factual information in isolated form. Instead write objectives that require learners to apply factual information as needed to perform job tasks.

- Facts can be displayed using statements, diagrams with descriptive tables, lists, and charts.

- In manuals, flag factual information by writing unique marginal labels that summarize the information conveyed by the facts.

• On computers, use color, fonts, and indentation to display factual information clearly. Use prompts to avoid lecture frames and windows to display information about diagrams.

• When designing practice for factual information, either in manuals or on computer, make use of job aids. Provide mnemonics and design exercises that require trainees to apply factual information to job-related tasks. Provide memory support by displaying facts in windows during CBT practice.

• Your tests should match your performance objectives, so avoid items that ask for recall of facts out of job context. Instead, design items matched to your lesson objective which will require the utilization of facts to complete tasks.

In Chapter 4, I described how to identify and teach concepts, one type of related information trainees need to know to effectively perform the procedures associated with their jobs. There is another category of supporting information that differs significantly from concepts: facts. Suppose you were training new credit representatives to classify customer credit status by evaluating applications and assigning a code. The code numbers ranged from 1 to 9 and represented various types of credit standings, from "unacceptable" to "VIP customer." To complete this task, the employee must know the code meanings. This is an example of factual information. Factual information is very different from concepts in its characteristics and in how our memories process it. Teaching factual information requires instructional techniques different from those used for concepts.

In this chapter I'll describe how facts differ from concepts so you can identify factual information in your training program. We will then look at guidelines for the effective display of factual information in workbooks and on computer screens. Because facts can only be processed at the remember level, they are inefficient in terms of memory storage capacity and retrieval. We will discuss alternative ways to help trainees access the factual information they need for job performance, while reducing the load on human memory as much as possible. Design of practice exercises to by-pass memory demands will be described for classroom and computer use. Last, I will describe ways of verifying that your trainees have successfully acquired the factual information they need to do their jobs.

WHAT IS FACTUAL INFORMATION?

Figure 5–1 illustrates the differences between concepts and facts. In Chapter 4, I described concepts as groups of objects or ideas that are given a common name, such as "chair," "mammal," "house." Within each concept class are individual examples that share the common characteristics of the class but which also vary on a number of features irrelevant to the basic concept. For example, all chairs have a back and seat but may vary in color, material, presence of arms, etc. Unlike concepts, in which all members of the group share common properties, facts are unique, one-of-a-kind types of information.

Types of Facts

There are two categories of factual information: *singular facts* and *fact statements*. A singular fact is any object for which every occurrence is identical to every other occurrence. For example, Purchase Order Form 19–32A is used to order all office equipment. Since every Form 19–32A is just like every other Form 19–32A, it represents factual information. Most singular facts tend to be concrete in nature, including specific computer screens, forms, and unique equipment.

A fact statement involves unique associations among concepts. For example, the statement "Our recent purchase order requested 534 chairs" would be an association between the concepts of 534, chairs, and a purchase order. Other examples of fact statements could include: "The corporate assets total $45,000,000" or "Credit Code 3 represents customers with prior credit standing in our service territory" or "The new Vice President of Marketing is John Jones." Note that all of these statements represent unique associations among concepts. You would have no independent way to derive them.

Concepts are an efficient way to store knowledge. Once you have abstracted the common features of a concept such as

FIGURE 5–1 **Concepts Versus Facts: A Comparison**

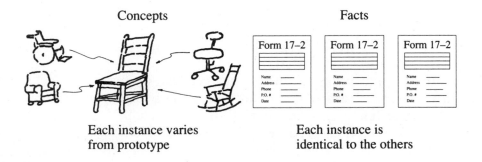

Concepts   Facts

Each instance varies   Each instance is
from prototype   identical to the others

FIGURE 5–2 **Memory Storage of Concepts Versus Facts**

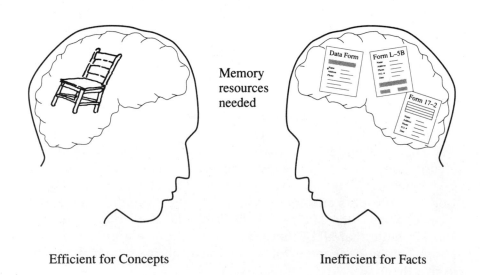

Memory
resources
needed

Efficient for Concepts   Inefficient for Facts

chair, you will recognize as chairs things you have never seen before. This is because you hold in memory the common features in a prototypic representation of the concept — an abstraction of "chairness." Unfortunately, facts must each be held in memory individually. This is because they have no common group features. By definition, a fact is a unique piece of information which must be individually memorized to be known. Compared to concepts, facts are a much more inefficient form of knowledge to store.

Identifying Factual Information

The job procedures you are training always have related technical information associated with them. Most of this supporting information is either conceptual or factual. Because technical experts are so familiar with the associated information, it is likely to have become unconscious knowledge. It is important to take a careful look at the steps in your procedures to identify all technical concepts and facts your trainees will need to do the procedure successfully. Because they are taught differently, you will need to distinguish between concepts and facts.

For example, look at the computer procedural training in Figure 3–6 on page 51. In this lesson the trainee is learning how to enter the correct transaction code to begin an accounting task. A trainee new to use of computers would need to know the concept of "transaction code." You would provide a definition such as "a transaction code is a four-letter key used to access various screens needed to accomplish different accounting tasks." Then the specific meaning of each transaction code such as "*AOCC* is used to open the cash drawer" would be the factual information associated with this procedure. Note that transaction code is a concept because there are multiple different transaction codes which all share common features. However, the meaning of each individual transaction code is unique and must be individually known. These meanings are examples of factual information.

When looking at your procedures to identify concepts or facts, ask yourself, "Are there multiple examples of this information that share common features but vary on irrelevant features?" If yes, you are dealing with a concept. Or, "Is this a unique piece of information?" If yes, you are dealing with factual information.

CHECK YOUR UNDERSTANDING

To be sure you can distinguish facts from concepts, try the short exercise on page 243.

Learning Facts at the Remember Level only

If you refer to the matrix diagram on page 30, you will note that all types of content can be processed at the remember and application levels except for facts. Factual information is unique because it can only be memorized. This means that factual information can only be held "as is" in memory; it cannot be transformed as can the other types of content. We all apply factual information every day in conjunction with the other types of content at the application level. But the facts themselves can only be held in memory in an untransformed state.

For example, consider the credit-code training we described earlier. Employees must assign a credit code to customers to classify their credit standing. In order to do that they must know the meaning of each code, which is factual. When evaluating the credit application, the employee assigns a code based on the customer data provided and the meaning of the code. The employee must apply criteria to decide which code to assign. In fact, the action being taken by the employee is really a procedure, and the training would use a decision table like the ones shown in Chapter 3. In order to make the decision, the employee must have available the factual information regarding the meanings of the codes. Thus, although facts themselves can only be held in memory, they are used in conjunction with other types of information, such as procedures, at the application level.

Because facts can only be processed at the remember level, they are very inefficient forms of information. As illustrated in Figure 5–3, that's because retrieval of information from human memory can be difficult. There is an unproductive tendency to require trainees to memorize too much information in many training programs. This is an unfortunate heritage from our earlier educational experiences when we devoted many hours to memory work. In business and industrial training our goal is to quickly build employees' confidence at performing their job tasks — not get them to memorize

FIGURE 5-3 Retrieval of Factual Information can be a Challenge

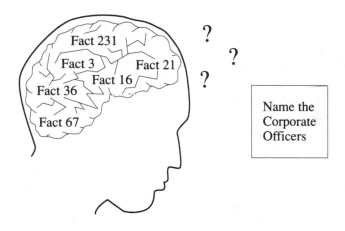

a lot of information. Therefore, when I describe ways to train facts, I will emphasize techniques you can use to bypass memory limitations and speed up the learning process.

Learning Objectives and Factual Information

Since facts can only be processed at the remember level, objectives written for factual information are remember-level objectives. For example, the credit code lesson would have an objective such as: "You will state the meaning of each credit code." The lesson on computer transaction codes would include an objective such as: "For every computer function, you will write the code needed to access that function."

However, to know the meanings of the credit codes as a separate objective is not necessary, and puts too much stress on memorization. Instead, write your objective at the lesson task level which would require knowledge of the facts to complete. For the computer codes, your learning objective would read: "For every function on this list, access the correct screen by entering the right transaction code." Here the objective is written at the procedural level but its performance would require the trainee to have access to the factual information. Your goal is to minimize employee memorization of facts and get them to actively use those facts in conjunction with their job tasks. Your objective for the procedures in the credit code lesson might read: "You will be given ten customer application forms and will be asked to assign the correct code to each one." In order to achieve this objective, the trainee would have to know the code meanings.

In conclusion, avoid writing separate learning objectives for factual information. Instead, incorporate the factual knowledge needed into the overall lesson task objective.

TRAINING FACTS: INFORMATIONAL INSTRUCTIONAL TECHNIQUES

As mentioned in Chapter 1, instructional methods include two major subsets: providing information, and designing practice exercises for acquiring the content at the appropriate level of performance. An assessment is designed as follow-up to make sure that trainees have reached the objective. In this section I will illustrate how to teach factual information, with formatting suggestions for workbook and computer displays. Then I will discuss the design of factual information practice, with an emphasis on ways to bypass unnecessary memorization, or, if memorization is necessary, how to best support retrieval of facts.

Providing Factual Information

Because concepts have key features and multiple examples, the basic instructional methods for teaching them include providing definitions that state the key features, along with examples and non-examples to help the trainee abstract critical from irrelevant features. But facts are unique, and therefore each must be fully presented in an individual display. Depending on the amount and type of factual information you have, you can use a variety of presentation displays, including fact statements, diagrams with descriptive tables, lists, tables, and charts. I will briefly describe these displays, then illustrate some formatting techniques for manuals and computer.

Fact Statements   When teaching facts, statements present the fact in a succinct sentence. For example: "Corporate assets totaled $45,000,000 in 1988." Or: "Mary Smith will assume duties of Marketing Vice President in April.

Diagrams with Descriptive Data   If you are dealing with a singular fact, such as a type of form or equipment, use an illustration to communicate its appearance so the trainee will recognize it. If the diagram has parts, use labels or key-points with an accompanying description table or windows to summarize the functions. We'll look at some examples in the next section.

Lists, Tables, Charts   Often you will have a number of related facts to present. If so, group them in the form of lists to present a series, or tables if you have descriptive information associated with each fact. In the credit code example, a two-column table would list each code number in one column and the code meaning in an adjacent column. If you want to illustrate relationships among a number of facts, such as reporting relationships in a department, an organizational chart is recommended.

Formatting of Facts in Training Manuals

Let's look at some ways to effectively format fact statements, diagrams, lists, or tables in a training manual.

Fact Sentences   Sentences are usually brief and presented in conjunction with another type of content, such as concepts or procedures. Figure 5–4 is taken from the toothbrushing lesson. This part of the lesson is presenting the concept of toothbrush. Recall that concepts are presented by providing definitions, examples, and non-examples, which are labeled as such in the margin. Look at the text at the bottom of the page that goes with the label "ownership." This is an example of a fact sentence.

Note that while you use *generic* marginal labels for concepts (i.e., they are always definitions, examples, non-examples), facts have *unique* labels. Because facts are one-of-a-kind information, a specific label of one to three words that summarizes the content of the statement will best help the reader retrieve the information when scanning the document. You will need to make up your own label that succinctly communicates the factual information. For example, Figure 5–5 is a lesson on a bill register. It is important that employees using the register be aware of its printing schedule. The schedule is presented in a fact sentence which is labeled "Printing Schedule." Making up effective and succinct labels requires some practice.

FIGURE 5–4 Format of Fact Statements in Training Manuals

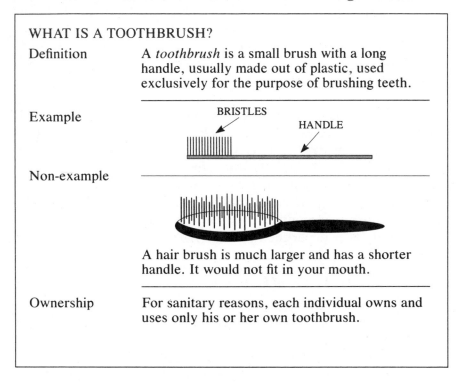

WHAT IS A TOOTHBRUSH?

Definition	A *toothbrush* is a small brush with a long handle, usually made out of plastic, used exclusively for the purpose of brushing teeth.
Example	BRISTLES HANDLE
Non-example	A hair brush is much larger and has a shorter handle. It would not fit in your mouth.
Ownership	For sanitary reasons, each individual owns and uses only his or her own toothbrush.

Formats for Singular Facts   Most job procedures involve a variety of singular facts, such as forms, computer screens, and equipment. When teaching concrete facts, provide a diagram of the form or equipment. When presenting forms or computer screens, reduce standard-size copies to make quick illustrations that can be pasted into your manual. For equipment, line art is generally better than photographs because it is cleaner and eliminates extraneous information.

With the illustration you may want to indicate parts or sections of the equipment or form, and describe their purpose. Although you can label the illustration, a lot of labels can be more confusing than helpful. Instead, consider keypointing the diagram and adding a descriptive table that summarizes the parts and/or functions. Figure 5–6 presents the component names and purposes associated with a SHARP FAX machine. Figure 5–7 from a lesson on estab-

FIGURE 5–5 Writing Meaningful Marginal Labels for Fact Statements

WHAT IS A REGULAR BILL REGISTER?

Introduction	The Regular Bill Register is used to obtain information regarding a customer's account. It is especially useful if the customer's bill has been corrected, or if the customer was billed more than once in the regular billing period. CIS reflects the total correction of the customer's bill, but the Bill Register will provide you with a more complete breakdown.
Definition	The REGULAR BILL REGISTER is a microfiche that is prepared for each cycle and book immediately following that cycle's regularly scheduled read date. It contains the current billing information and any activity that has taken place on the account since the previous billing.
Printing Schedule	The Regular Bill Register is printed daily by group cycle and district, and is a continuous print of the complete cycle. The bill register prints the same day that the customer's bill is mailed.
Re-design March 84	The Regular Bill Register format was redesigned in March 1984, and is now very similar to formats as shown on CIS.
Example	Regular Bill Register in use prior to March 1984:

abcdefg hijklmnop BB 51-29-500									BILL REGISTER	
	abcdefg hijklmnop		abcdefg hijklmnop	abcdefg hijklmnop	klmn defh	abcdefg hijklmn	tuvwxyzab cdef	tuvwxyzab cdef	xyzabtuvw hiklf	zabtuvw hiklf
banjituvwxfy		banjituvwxfy		hijklmoo pqrst	klmn defh	abcdefg hijklmn	abcdefg hijklmn	abcdefg hijklmn	defgabc lmnhjk	defgabc lmnhjk	xzstabc lmwadjk
				fghi bklmnove	klmn defh	abcdefg hijklmn	abcdefg mnors	tuvwxyzab cdef	tuvzabwxy cdef	uvzabw cdef
32	617	29	635	CM 191		01.28	51432	46.45	8.78753		CLI
29	602	33	630	.80		12.29	50867	48.78		
16	314	30	614	91385						
WH	2/		WT	RES	LS	W	S/P O	240 LKWR	240	LREV
AC	/		RES	#W			#NT	WCNKWR	345	NREV

FIGURE 5–6 Fact Diagram Display with Descriptive Table

MAJOR FAX COMPONENTS

Diagram of
SHARP FAX
Machine and
Components

This is a diagram of the SHARP FAX machine. The numbered parts correspond to the part descriptions listed below.

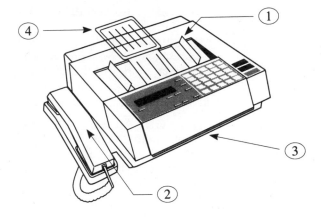

Part #	Name of Part	Purpose/Description
1	Adjustable guide	Set to width of document
2	Handset (phone)	Transmits and receives document data
3	Original document exit	Original document exits here
4	Document hopper	Supports long size documents

FIGURE 5–7 Fact Diagram Display with Descriptive Table

THE PAYMENT RECORD SCREEN

Diagram:
Payment
Record
Screen

PAYMENT HISTORY SUMMARY SCREEN

MS. MARGARET JONES

453-98-5786

JANUARY	OD	•• JULY	W
FEBRUARY	PP	AUGUST	PIF
MARCH	W	SEPTEMBER	PIF
•• APRIL	W	OCTOBER	
MAY	PIF	NOVEMBER	
JUNE	—	DECEMBER	

Parts of the
Payment
Record
Screen

Part	Field Name	Purpose
1	Name	The name of the customer whose social security number is on application
2	SSN	Customer's social security number
3	Bullets	•• indicate a warning notice was sent
4	Month	Month of billing
5	Payment	Type of payment received

Symbol	Meaning
PIF	Paid in Full
PP	Partial Payment
OD	Overdue Notice issued
W	Warning Notice issued

lishing customer credit presents a payment record screen accompanied by a table that provides the field names and purpose.

Presenting Multiple Facts   Often your trainees will need access to a series of facts, such as the meanings of Credit Codes 1–9. Aggregate your factual information into tables or lists for efficient clean presentation. In our toothbrushing lesson, when presenting the concept of toothpaste, the instructor used a bulleted list to provide information about various brands. Note the marginal label in Figure 5–8 that the instructor created. Note also that factual information can be inserted anywhere in a lesson where the

FIGURE 5–8 **Display of Several Facts Using Bulleted List**

WHAT IS TOOTHPASTE?

Definition   *Toothpaste* is a type of soap which has a pleasant taste, usually comes in a tube, and is squeezed out. It comes in various colors (but is often white) and has a creamy consistency.

Example

Tube   Paste

Brands   There are many brands of toothpaste, such as:

• Crest

• Gleam

• Pepsodent

Non-example

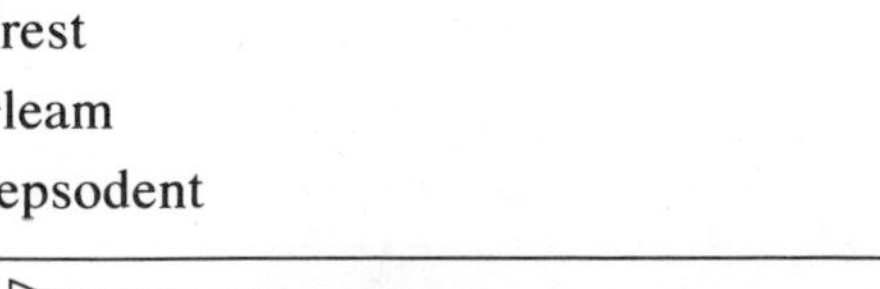

Other products come in tubes that are not for use in the mouth. They will not be labelled "paste."

information logically fits. Thus, facts often support lessons about concepts, procedures, or the other content types we will see in the later chapters. Short factual sections such as the list of toothpaste brands are typically inserted in the middle of a larger lesson on the concept or procedure being trained. Longer factual sections, such as diagrams with descriptive tables, may require a separate page, such as Figure 5–6.

In the section on singular facts, some examples of tables to support diagrams were shown. Tables may also stand alone, especially where you have information about a number of related facts. Refer back to Figure 5–7. The major purpose of the table is to explain the parts of the payment record screen. Look however at key-point 5. Here an embedded fact table is used to summarize the meanings of the different symbols on the computer screen.

Acronyms are a very common type of factual information in all major organizations. New employees feel immediately confused when they hear phrases like: "Be sure not to classify the DFDs with the ARGs unless the LFs have been ODed." All acronyms associated with common tasks should be presented early in the training. Figure 5–9 illustrates a lesson on new equipment-testing processes that presents the various acronyms associated with the work groups involved.

Formatting Facts on Computer

Factual information can be formatted for computer, using many of the same displays used for manuals. Fact statements, tables, diagrams, and lists are all recommended. However, due to screen size restrictions, you may not want to use marginal labels as on 8½"-by-11"-page. Figure 5–10 illustrates some factual information organized into tabular format. Depending on the number of levels in a factual hierarchy, you could use color, different fonts, and/or indentations to cleanly display the information. This example illustrates displays of factual information for reference purposes more than for training. Reference material placed on the computer is called computer-based reference, or CBR. CBR is likely to become a major application as software systems evolve to handle reference functions. As information becomes obsolete, a computer reference document can be quickly updated, replacing prior versions automatically.

FIGURE 5–9 Acronyms Displayed in Fact Table

WHO ARE THE KEY PLAYERS

Introduction   As in the other phases, many groups are involved
in burn-in. Most have acronyms. The multitude of
acronyms may at first seem like a barrier to getting
your job done.

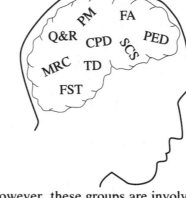

In fact, however, these groups are involved to help
you and are the means by which equipment is
successfully transferred.

Acronyms   The acronyms for the groups involved in burn-in
are as follows:

ACRONYM	Full name
PM	Program Manager
PED	Process Equipment Development
CPD	Components Plant Development
MRC	Equipment Review Committee
FST	Factory Segment Team
TD	Technology Development
FA	Factory Automation
Q&R	Quality & Reliability
SCS	Strategic Capability Segment

FIGURE 5–10 **Factual Information Displayed for Computer Reference**

Product Specifications:
2-23-89

Zappers
  Only red and yellow in stock
  Price increase projected Q3
CAT. Ref:
  2–142 .... $13.99

Zingers
  32″ and 45″ length in stock
  Sale price through Q2

CAT. Ref:
  2–231 .... $192.95

Integrating Reference and Training into Automated Systems
Some new computer software products integrate reference help as well as training options into the actual production system. Figure 5–11 provides a simplified illustration of how this might work. Suppose a new operator is evaluating a payment history screen. A help-function key can access reference information such as code meanings or decision criteria. Or, if more in-depth information is desired, the operator can move from the application directly into training on how to use the screen to establish customer credit.

In the design of factual displays for computer applications, space restrictions indicate the use of a window overlaid on the diagram to illustrate parts. In Figure 5–12A, a bulleted list states the four main panels of the software being trained. Figure 5–12B presents a factual diagram illustrating the home screen. To explain more about the screen, a window is overlaid in 5–12C that presents details about some of the screen codes.

Using Prompts for Interactive Fact Instruction   For training purposes, you can make teaching of factual information on computer much more interesting by turning a fact-lecture–type frame into an interactive screen. You do this by showing an illustration of the factual information and asking a question about it on the same screen. Figure 5–13A shows first a lecture frame followed by a recall question. This type of frame, known as a copy frame, requires very little mental processing by the learner, and thus results in little or no learning. Figure 5–13B shows how to make this a more interactive and interesting teaching point by using a prompted

FIGURE 5–11 Embedding Reference and Training in Computer Applications

PAYMENT HISTORY SUMMARY SCREEN

MRS. MARGARET JONES

453-98-5786

JANUARY	OD	•• JULY	W
FEBRUARY	PP	AUGUST	PIF
MARCH	W	SEPTEMBER	PIF
•• APRIL	W	OCTOBER	
MAY	PIF	NOVEMBER	
JUNE	—	DECEMBER	

PF 1 = QUIT   PF 3 = MAIN MENU   PF 5 = HELP

Application Screen

Pf 5: Help Request by Operator

HELP FOR PAYMENT HISTORY SCREEN

Move cursor to help feature wanted and press enter

CODE MEANINGS, HIGHLIGHT CODE: OD   W

PP   P1 F

CREDIT CRITERIA

TRAINING ON HOW TO USE THIS SCREEN

PF 1 = QUIT   PF 3 = MAIN MENU   PF 5 = RETURN

Embedded Reference/Training Menu Screen

FIGURE 5–12 Examples of Three Factual Displays Used to Train Computer Software Application

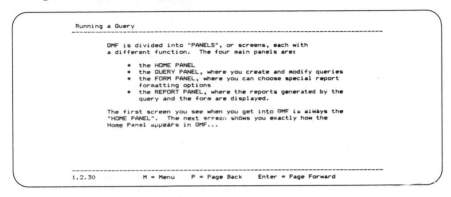

A.   Bulleted List Overview of Application

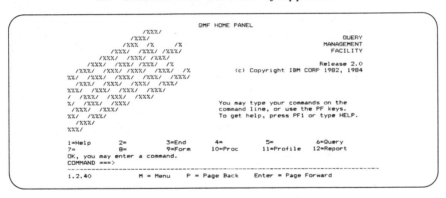

B.   Diagram of One Panel

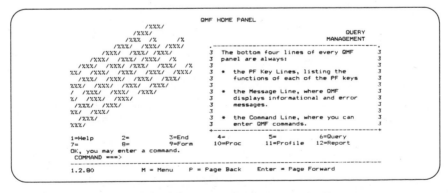

C.   Use of Window to Summarize Code Meanings

Reproduced with Permission The Courseware Developers.

FIGURE 5–13 **Use of Prompts for Fact Training**

Introductory Sales Training   Lesson 2

To be valid, all sales tickets must have:
• price of item
• inventory code (7 characters)
• store code (2 digits)

A–1.   Factual Content in a Lecture Frame

Introductory Sales Training   Lesson 2

What 3 items must appear on all valid sales tickets:

1. _____

2. _____

3. _____

A–2.   Recall Frame Based on Lecture Frame

Introductory Sales Training   Lesson 2

What 3 items can be found on all sales tickets?

Store 67
A259687

$19.99

_____

_____

_____

B.   Instead, Use a Prompted Question Frame

question frame. The prompted question frame forces the learner to look at the prompt, a sales ticket in this case, and evaluate it in order to respond to the question. This will increase the probability of learning the information.

Displaying Multiple Facts If you are dealing with many facts, you might want to consider using another medium than computer to present them. Unless you are specifically developing a computer-based reference application, it would be better to display large volumes of factual information on paper, which could be read along with CBT or separately. This is because it is tedious and uninteresting to read through screen after screen of factual information. Still, all training will include some factual information. Present it cleanly in your CBT followed promptly by practice which encourages the student to use the facts to complete a job task.

This brings us to the next major event of learning: design of practice exercises. Because facts can only be processed at the remember level, they present some unique challenges. The next section will describe practice techniques to use with factual information.

TRAINING FACTS: INSTRUCTIONAL TECHNIQUES FOR PRACTICE

When designing practice for factual information, first consider why the employee needs the factual information and under what circumstances. Since facts can only be held in memory, assimilation of large numbers of facts is inefficient and boring. Three alternatives to bypass memorization of facts are:

1. provide job aids and design practice on the use of them.
2. provide mnemonic cues for retrieval of facts that must be memorized.
3. design practice that requires the trainee to access facts in conjunction with the task being trained.

Let's look at each of these in more detail.

Provide Job Aids to Bypass Memorization of Factual Information In most cases facts are used to help perform a procedure. For example, the employee needs to know the meaning of the nine credit codes in order to classify customer credit applications.

FIGURE 5–14 Typical Job Aids Used to Bypass Memory of Factual Information

Example 1 — Pocket Guide for Use of Hand-Held Terminal in Field

Getting Information from Your DATACAP Terminal

To Find Out	DEPRESS Key Marked	This Many Times
SERVICE ADDRESS	ADDR	ONCE
ACCOUNT NUMBER	ADDR	TWICE
CUSTOMER NAME	NAME	ONCE
METER NUMBER	METER NUMBER	ONCE
MAXIMUM DEMAND	METER NUMBER	TWICE

Example 2 — Determining Which Claim Form to Use

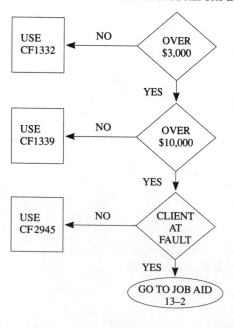

Rather than memorizing them, the employee could perform the task just as well by looking up the codes on a card. Recall that job aids such as cards are intended to be used during actual job performance. Such job aids are becoming more common because they help the employee perform his work consistently and efficiently and in some cases may even bypass the need for training.

Job aids take many forms. Some common examples for use with computer applications are cards that list codes, templates to put over the keyboards with key functions listed, or help screens built into the system. Figure 5–14 illustrates some simple job aids.

More sophisticated job aids can provide procedural directions. Many copy machines show animated displays that walk the employee through basic problem resolution procedures, such as clearing paper jams or adding more paper. In this way, training on solving simple copy machine problems can be avoided. Airline pilots usually check off standard takeoff tasks using a checklist as a safety measure to be sure routine procedures are followed consistently. Almost all training programs should design job aids as part of the training. It will help insure the transfer of the training to the job since the job aid is used at the work station. Part of the training should be devoted to getting the worker using the job aid to perform job tasks. When job aids are included with CBT lessons, mention them early in the lesson and create exercises that require the learner to use them.

FIGURE 5–15 **Job Aid Built into Copy Machine**

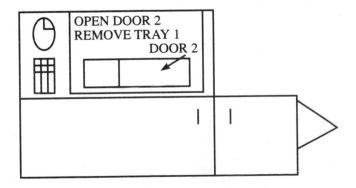

Provide Mnemonics when Memory of Facts is Essential
There are occasions, however, when it is essential that the employee memorize factual information to successfully execute job tasks, and it may be undesirable to use a job aid. Certain sales situations may call for a smooth delivery of product benefits without reference to job aids. Or employees may have to respond quickly or work in environmental conditions which preclude the use of job aids. For example, some manufacturing processes require sterile, dust-free environments where extraneous materials must be limited. If memory of factual information is essential, consider the use of mnemonics.

Mnemonics are basically memory supports that involve an association between familiar and new knowledge so that the factual knowledge can be called up with the familiar. Many piano players recall the Every-Good-Boy-Does-Fine mnemonic used to remember scales. A well known electronic sequence to remember the numeric value of color bands on resistors is "*bad boys rape our young girls, but violet gives willingly.*" This represents black, brown, red, orange, yellow, green, blue, violet, gray, and white.

Association mnemonics can be used to memorize more isolated facts. For example, if you wanted a mnemonic for the fact that Nakasone was Premier of Japan, what visual association could you make between the unknown Nakasone and Japan? One idea is to imagine yourself knocking on a Sony television set. Knock a Sony = Nakasone, and Sony links to Japan.

FIGURE 5–16 Using Visual Associations as Mnemonics

1. Think of a familiar image that the unknown fact sounds like

2. The image must link to the meaning of the unknown

NAKASONE sounds like:

KNOCK   AND   SONY

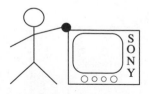

LINKS TO JAPAN

Design Practice for Application of Related Skills — Not Factual Memorization   Recall the example of the nine credit codes I mentioned at the beginning of the chapter. Rather than asking the trainee to list the meaning of each code, design practice that requires use of the procedure. That is, give the trainees customer scenarios and ask them what code to assign. This will provide practice on the factual information, as the trainee will need to access it in order to perform the task.

Design of Practice for Classroom Manuals

Use the guidelines listed above to design workbook exercises that require trainees to apply factual information as needed on the job. Figure 5–17 shows an effective practice exercise in which trainees are classifying customer credit status. To perform this task, knowledge of the meaning of the screen codes is needed. These are provided on a job aid and the class practice exercise asks the trainee to use the job aid to classify sample credit scenarios.

A major computer chip manufacturing company uses complex specialized equipment in their manufacturing process. Trainers felt it was essential that new equipment operators know the correct terms for the equipment parts in order to communicate problems accurately to service engineers over the telephone. You could design an exercise like the one in Figure 5–18A that asks learners to fill in the names of the parts. Better, however, would be an exercise that depicted a malfunction and required the trainee to describe it precisely enough for another trainee to locate it, such as the exercise in Figure 5–18B. This exercise would be more related to the context of the job than the fill-in-the-blank example.

In short, when faced with a training program filled with substantial factual information, use a creative approach to get employees using the facts for the job-related purposes for which they are intended. Now let's take a look at practice for computer-based training programs.

Design of Practice for Computer-Based Training

Use as many of the principles described above for design of CBT practice. The credit-rating exercises could be directly translated to CBT. The equipment terminology exercise, however, would have to be modified to accommodate the requirement for structured questions. Along with a depicted equipment problem, you could

FIGURE 5–17 Design Practice to Help Trainee Learn to Use Job Aid

PRACTICE 3: CLASSIFYING CUSTOMER CREDIT STATUS

For each customer payment record, decide if the payment history is good or poor. Use your job aid to interpret the screens.

1.

PAYMENT HISTORY SUMMARY SCREEN

MR. SAM SMITH

JANUARY	PIF	JULY	PP
FEBRUARY	PP	AUGUST	PIF
•• MARCH	W	SEPTEMBER	PIF
APRIL	PIF	OCTOBER	
MAY	PIF	NOVEMBER	
JUNE	—	DECEMBER	

Credit Status: _____

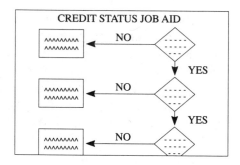

insert a diagram like the one shown in Figure 5–19, where the trainee would fill in the blanks related to the malfunction depicted.

Suppose you are training an on-line computer application. You may want trainees to learn to use special function keys which are assigned specific purposes. After presenting the functions of the keys either on the screen or on a job aid, rather than ask the trainees to identify the function of key X, you could ask them to select the function key that accesses the help screen, for example. A correct response should result in a simulation of the actual system by bringing up the help screen along with a correct-answer feedback message, as in Figures 5–20A and 5–20B.

On-Line Memory Support   Providing memory support for factual information is even more important in computer-based training than in workbooks, because it may not be easy to retrieve

FIGURE 5–18 Designing Practice Exercise for Factual Information

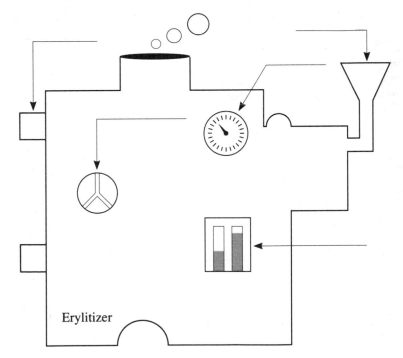

Practice 5: Parts of the Erylitizer

Fill in the blank with the name of the Erylitizer part indicated:

Erylitizer

A. *Recall of factual information out of context of its use.*

Practice 5: Describing the Parts of the Erylitizer

You note the pressure gauge on the Erylitizer looks like the diagram on the right. The parts are showing fragmentation on their lateral surfaces. Describe your problem to the engineer using the correct technical terms.

B. *Use of factual information in realistic job context.*

FIGURE 5–19 Design of Practice for Computer-Based Training

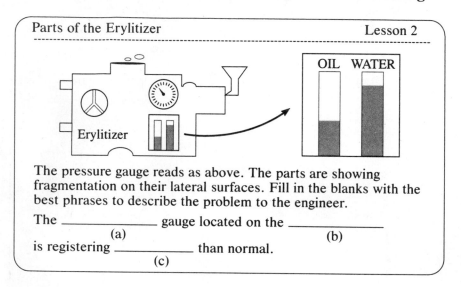

Parts of the Erylitizer   Lesson 2

OIL   WATER

Erylitizer

The pressure gauge reads as above. The parts are showing
fragmentation on their lateral surfaces. Fill in the blanks with the
best phrases to describe the problem to the engineer.

The _____ gauge located on the _____
            (a)   (b)
is registering _____ than normal.
                      (c)

FIGURE 5–20 Simulate Actual System Response for Feedback

Using CARS System   Lesson 3

Now suppose while you were adding inventory you forgot what
units went into the AMT field. To get help you would press the
function key designed for help. Try it now.

A.   Instead of asking which PF key brings up help.

Using CARS System   Lesson 3

HELP SCREEN
The AMT field requires dollars and cents entered like this:
42.3 or 42. (zeros will be automatically added).

> Good Work. PF 5 brings up help
> related to the field you are
> working on.

B.   Feedback simulates real system response.

FIGURE 5–21 **Placement of Facts in Windows for Memory Support**

Assigning Loan Limits		Lesson 3

For each customer described below, decide whether you would approve the requested loan.

credit code	loan limit
2	$1,000
3	$5,000
5	$20,000

Mary Smith is single with no dependents. She earns $26,000 annually and has major debts of mortgage and car payments of $1,200 monthly. She has applied for a $10,000 loan. Would you approve? _____

the facts in the CBT. Therefore, during CBT practice where trainees are asked to perform a task that requires access to factual information, provide a window containing a factual summary as a memory support. Figure 5–21 shows an example from a CBT course on approval of customer loans.

In summary, whenever creating practice around use of factual information, ask yourself: "How will the trainees be using these facts?" Then design the practice to require the trainees to use the facts to complete the job task for which they are needed rather than to memorize the factual information in isolation.

Evaluating Learning Results

Once you have designed some practice exercises that require trainees to use the factual information needed to complete job tasks, you have a good format for design of test items to evaluate instructional effectiveness. Your test items, like your practice exercises, should be realistic simulations, using the factual information as it would be used on the job. In fact, when designing practice exercises, create some additional items similar in format to be used on your test.

Be sure that your test includes some items that make use of the job aid you have designed so you can verify that the trainees can effectively access the information provided on it.

PREVIEW OF CHAPTER SIX

In Chapters 3–5, I have given the techniques for teaching basic job procedures and providing the related technical information needed to perform them successfully. The focus has been on teaching the information employees need to perform job-related tasks. Sometimes, however, in order to complete a task, the employee needs to know about how something works. Knowing how things work can be essential to working effectively with or on those things. For example, doing maintenance on equipment may require knowing the overall functioning of the various parts of the equipment.

Any information that depicts how things work is called a process. In Chapter 6, I will distinguish processes from procedures and indicate when and how to teach them.

The Content-Performance Matrix: Processes

	Facts	Concepts	Processes	Procedures	Principles
Apply	////////	Classify new Examples *Which file name is valid?* *A. 043MYFILE* *B. MYFILE9*	**Solve A Problem** **Make An Inference** *Customer asks about his bill. Where should you check first?*	Perform the Procedure *Log onto the Computer*	
Remember	Remember the Facts *What is your computer password?*	Remember the Definition *Define Valid File Name*	**Remember the Stages** *Describe How Work Orders Are Processed*	Remember the Steps *List the Steps to Log onto the Computer*	

CHAPTER 6

How to Teach Processes

CHAPTER SUMMARY

- Processes are descriptions of how things work. There are two basic types of processes: business (describing work flows in organizations) and technical (describing how things work in equipment- or natural systems).

- Learning about processes results in knowing how things like manufacturing operations, corporate functions, chemical reactions or computer programs work, rather than how to do things.

- Processes may be included in your lessons as background or "nice-to-know" information, or they may provide knowledge essential to effective job performance. If process knowledge is essential, you will need to write learning objectives for processes at the application level.

- At the remember level, trainees recall the major stages of the process as provided in the instruction.

- At the application level, trainees can solve a problem or make an inference based on their knowledge of how the process works.

- Informational displays for processes include process tables and flow diagrams. Flow diagrams are preferred as they are more memorable and more efficient. Sometimes diagrams and tables can be effectively used together to display process information.

- Processes can be displayed on computer effectively through use of animation and color to illustrate the dynamic nature of the process. Simulations of the process allow the learner to interact with it.

- If the process is being presented as background information for a procedure lesson, and therefore has no accompanying learning objective, practice may not be needed. But if an understanding of the process is important to performance of the procedure, design practice at the application level.

- Practice at the application level asks trainees to solve a problem or make an inference based on the process. This can be done via case studies, simulations, or work problems.

- If you have written a learning objective for the process, you can measure learner achievement by designing test questions that match your instructional objective and your practice exercises.

In Chapters 3–5, I described techniques for identifying and teaching most of the core-content types of technical training: procedures and their related concepts and facts. Often employees or company departments routinely complete their job tasks without an understanding of the bigger picture of which their work is a part. This lack of perspective can result in sub-optimal work performance. Quality improvement programs emphasize the need to define the processes whereby products are produced in an organization. A cross-functional perspective of product development is essential to defining points of potential quality improvement. This bigger perspective can be provided by teaching the business or technical process related to a specific product or service.

In this chapter I will define processes, distinguishing them from procedures. We will then look at guidelines for effective teaching of processes, including some sample formats for workbooks and computer. Processes can be psychologically processed at the Remember or Application level. As with other types of content, an emphasis on the Application level is recommended. I will describe practice exercises which encourage trainees to apply process knowledge not just memorize it. Last, I will provide some ideas for verifying that the trainee has acquired the process at the Application level.

WHAT ARE PROCESSES?

While procedures are directive in nature, *processes* are descriptive. Procedures tell employees how to go about doing a task, while processes tell them how something works. For example, a lesson on how a gasoline engine works would be a process lesson useful to a mechanic trainee. A lesson on how Company X hires new employees might be useful to a clerk processing some phases of hiring. A number of departments play roles in processes such as hiring: an individual employee working in personnel would follow his or her procedure which, along with procedures followed by employees in other departments, make up the hiring process.

Types of Processes

Processes can be classified into 2 categories:

- *business* systems depicting organizational work flows
- *technical* systems depicting stages in mechanical or natural systems

A business process consists of several stages performed by different employees or departments, resulting in achievement of an organizational goal. Employee hiring, customer billing, and panel assembly are examples. These processes are combinations of individual procedures performed by different employees or functional areas of the organization. By contrast, a technical process consists of stages that involve equipment operations or natural phenomena that accomplish a specific function. Some examples would include how a steam turbine works, how glopples are manufactured in the erylitizer, or how blood circulates.

Business processes are somewhat situational in that what may be a process in one setting could be a procedure in another. For example in a moderate to large company, new employee hiring is typically a process involving several departments. However in a small company, the hiring may be a procedure handled by a single individual. When you do your job analysis at the start of your training planning, you will be able to determine whether specific functions are processes or procedures in the setting you are analyzing. Technical processes do not have this situational character. They will always be classified as processes since they describe systems, such as equipment, that operate outside direct human control.

Motivational and Instructional Value of Processes   When an employee's work is part of an organizational system, an understanding of the process can support learning of job tasks, work motivation, and overall product quality. If, for example, the employee knows his internal customer — the recipient of his work product — is the accounting department, he will gain a more meaningful perspective of his role, along with the potential to define and improve work quality for his customers.

Often process knowledge contributes directly to a more meaningful application of procedures. If a programmer understands how the modules are interrelated for the system she is maintaining, her coding will be more effective than if she is working without that larger picture. If a technician is faced with a problem on some equipment, more effective troubleshooting will result from an understanding of the technical process whereby the equipment works.

Identifying the Processes in Your Training

As you look at the procedures you are about to train, ask yourself if they relate to a process. If you are training preventative maintenance of the erylitizer, it would be helpful to have a general understanding of how the erylitizer works. Figure 6–1 illustrates this technical process.

If you are teaching a new-hire to set up an investment plan on the computer, using information from a variety of forms, you might provide an overview of the investment process, showing where the various forms originate and what happens to them after the new-hire completes her part. Figure 6–2 illustrates this business process.

In previous chapters I have used a "How to Brush Your Teeth" lesson to illustrate techniques for teaching procedures, concepts,

FIGURE 6–1 How the Erylitizer Processes Glopples:

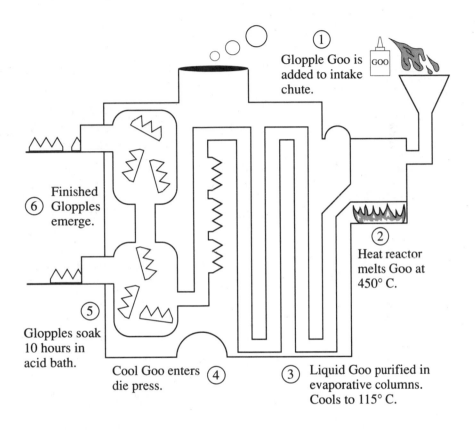

and facts. It might be useful to include a brief section on the process of tooth decay early in the lesson. This information should provide greater motivation for, and understanding of, the techniques for flossing and brushing. Figure 6–3 illustrates this natural process.

While a process may provide useful background information to a procedure lesson, sometimes the entire lesson or course focuses on a process. One company developed a lesson on the equipment transfer process that described how new equipment was selected, evaluated, burned in, and installed at a beta site prior to wide-scale implementation.

FIGURE 6–2 How Automatic Investment Plans Are Processed

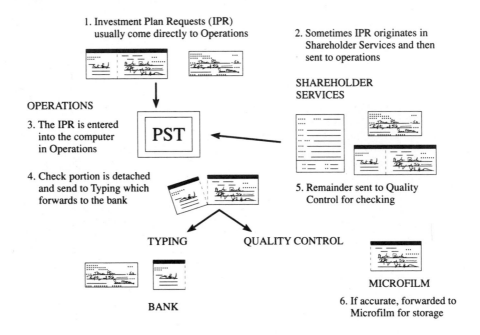

1. Investment Plan Requests (IPR) usually come directly to Operations

2. Sometimes IPR originates in Shareholder Services and then sent to operations

SHAREHOLDER SERVICES

OPERATIONS

3. The IPR is entered into the computer in Operations

PST

4. Check portion is detached and send to Typing which forwards to the bank

5. Remainder sent to Quality Control for checking

TYPING   QUALITY CONTROL

MICROFILM

BANK

6. If accurate, forwarded to Microfilm for storage

CHECK YOUR UNDERSTANDING

To be sure you can identify processes, try the short exercise on page 245.

Learning Processes At Remember and Application Levels

Except for facts, all the types of content can be processed at either the remember or application level. When learning processes at the remember level, the trainee is recalling or recognizing the basic steps or stages associated with the process. The medical trainee might describe the process of blood circulation through the heart and lungs. Note that the information is untransformed from the way it is presented in the lesson.

At the application level, the learner is able to solve a problem or make an inference based on the process. For example, the medical trainee might be asked: "What would happen if leakage between

FIGURE 6–3 How a Tooth Decays: A Process Summary

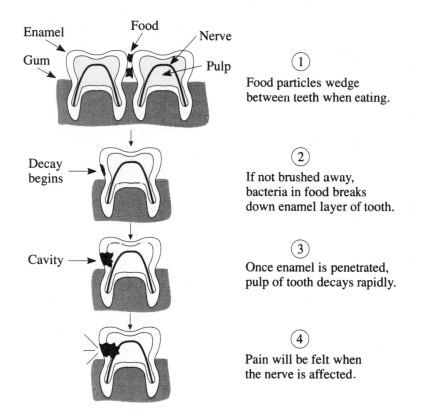

Enamel   Food   Nerve
Gum   Pulp

① Food particles wedge between teeth when eating.

Decay begins

② If not brushed away, bacteria in food breaks down enamel layer of tooth.

Cavity

③ Once enamel is penetrated, pulp of tooth decays rapidly.

④ Pain will be felt when the nerve is affected.

the left and right ventricle occurred?" Or: "What would be the effect of obstruction of the pulmonary artery?" To answer these questions, the trainee would need to apply knowledge about blood circulation to solve the problem.

Application of process knowledge is especially important for employees involved in any form of troubleshooting where they might have to resolve problems that occur in an overall process. Systematic problem solving in manufacturing operations begins by flow-charting the production process. Once the process is clearly defined, all employees associated with the process, from engineers to production workers, can brainstorm potential sources of the problem using cause and effect analysis.

Writing Process Learning Objectives at the Application Level

You may not always write a learning objective for the process part of your training. First ask yourself, "How critical is this process knowledge to the effective completion of job tasks?" If you feel that knowledge of the process is a "need-to-know," as opposed to a "nice-to-know," then establish a goal for this knowledge by writing a learning objective. Otherwise you might include the process in your training but not hold your trainees accountable for the knowledge.

If you write a learning objective, start out by defining for yourself how the process is tied into the trainee's job. Write an objective that asks the learner to apply the process knowledge to solve a job-related problem. Your objective for the erylitizer engineer might be: "You will be given descriptions of faulty glopples along with operator observations. Based on how the erylitizer works, you will define possible problems in the manufacturing process." A process-related objective for a customer service representative might state: "You will answer customer questions about credit-related documentation they have received and direct them to the correct department to resolve the situation." An objective for a programmer handling system maintenance might read: "You will be given specific program functions or problems and be asked to identify the program modules responsible."

TRAINING PROCESSES: INFORMATIONAL INSTRUCTIONAL TECHNIQUES

The design of all effective instruction involves providing clear information, giving practice with answers to help the learner assimilate the information, testing for achievement of the instructional objective, and repeating the teaching cycle as needed. In this section we will look at some techniques for displaying process information in workbooks and on computer. This will be followed by ideas for design of practice and test items.

Informational Techniques

Like procedures, processes involve a series of steps or stages that describe how something works or how something is done by several employees or departments. Use either process tables or flow diagrams to present the stages. Business processes usually involve information of the "who-does-what-when" type. Figure 6–4 shows

FIGURE 6–4 Sample Process Stage Table For Workbook

The Training Registration Process

Step	Action	Responsibility
1.	• Complete PROGRAM INFORMATION FORM. • Forward completed form to CTRS Administrator.	HRD Consultant
2.	• Enter program information into computer. • Inform clerk(s) of assigned class numbers and julian dates.	CTRS Administrator
3.	As 19–140s arrive for all programs. . . • Stamp 19–140s and fill in appropriate class number and julian date. • Enter participants' social security numbers into computer (NEW 19140). • As needed, enter changes to scheduled attendance of participants (NEW 19140).	Clerk Ref: NEW 19140
4.	Monthly, run reports of participants scheduled to attend programs.	CTRS Administrator
5.	Just prior to program start date. . . <table><tr><td>IF 19-140s. . .</td><td>THEN</td></tr><tr><td>*have* been received prior to program</td><td>• enter participants' social security numbers into computer (TRAINING). • print computerized participant list. • forward list to consultant.</td></tr><tr><td>have *not* been received prior to program</td><td>• give consultant TEMPORARY PARTICIPANT LIST form.</td></tr></table>	Clerk Ref: TRAINING

a process table that includes columns for steps, action, and responsibility. This example illustrates a process of registering trainees in which the consultant, administrator, and clerk all have a role. A table for a technical process that summarizes how equipment works might include columns for steps, parts, and description.

A second method of displaying processes is to use a flow diagram. The flow diagram depicting the processing of work orders in Figure 6–5 summarizes the various stages in the process. The diagrams may be circular to illustrate ongoing flows, or linear for processes with defined starts and stops. Figure 6–6 illustrates a more complex flow diagram linking two circular processes in the profit center and print shop. A slight variation on the flow diagram is illustrated in Figure 6–7 where a tree diagram summarizes the process tasks undertaken by the computer during an update transaction. An understanding of how the computer processes modules of software is useful to the programmer who will code the various modules. If you have a choice between the process table or the flow diagram, the diagram is preferable because the illustrations are

FIGURE 6–5 Sample Process Flow Diagram For Workbook

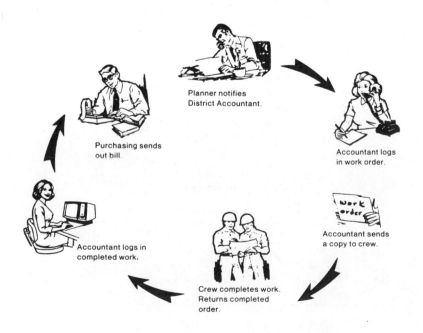

Planner notifies
District Accountant.

Purchasing sends
out bill.

Accountant logs
in work order.

Accountant logs in
completed work.

Accountant sends
a copy to crew.

Crew completes work.
Returns completed
order.

FIGURE 6–6 Sample Process Flow Diagram For Workbook

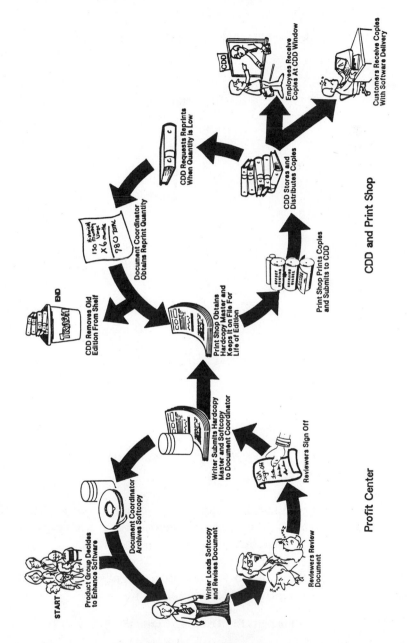

Document Maintenance Process

FIGURE 6–7 **Sample Process Tree Diagram For Workbook**

How Update Transactions Are Processed

Tasks executed when unique key entered

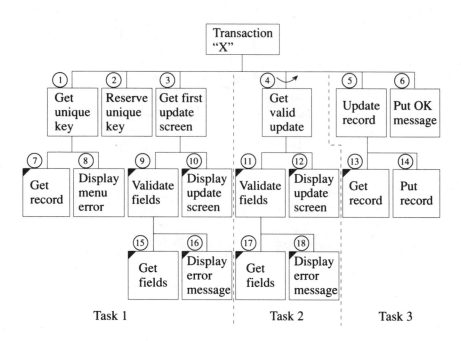

more memorable and more information can often be summarized in a short amount of space.

Combining Tables and Diagrams   Sometimes it is helpful to use the flow diagram as the primary illustration of the process and to add a table that provides supplementary descriptive information. Like the tables used to describe factual displays, you can key-point numbers in the table to the diagram. Figure 6–8 illustrates a diagram with a descriptive table to support it.

Formats for Training Manuals

The page layouts for process tables and flow diagrams are similar. The page heading should be left-justified and titled "How X's Are Processed" or "How the X Works." A brief introductory para-

FIGURE 6–8 Combining Diagrams and Tables For Processes

How Procurements Are Processed

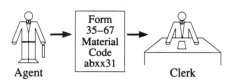

Agent   Clerk

Event	Description
1.	Procurement Agent receives Form 35–67
2.	Agent checks material code
3.	Agent forwards to clerk

graph might state the relevance of the process to the overall lesson. The process table or flow diagram should have an identifying marginal label such as "Work Order Process" or "Equipment Transfer Process." Figure 6–9 illustrates the work order process laid out on the page.

Formats for CBT

Presenting process information on computer is similar to presenting it in training manuals, in that the goal is to clearly depict each major stage involved. However, the formats might differ due to screen layout considerations and capabilities of color and animation. Figure 6–10 illustrates a very simple process lesson created with a mainframe authoring system. The lesson is designed to teach clerks how to process purchase orders. Before teaching the procedures, the overall process of purchase order preparation is presented. In this example, several screens are used to illustrate each major stage. As each screen presents a new stage, a summary of the prior stages is overlaid in the window at the top of the screen.

A process lesson delivered on computer could readily take advantage of both color and animation capabilities to illustrate the dynamic nature of stages, such as those illustrated in Figures 6–11 and 6–12. The blood circulation lesson could illustrate the flow of blood with compressions of the heart showing the oxygenated blood in bright red and deoxygenated blood in darker shades. Animated arrows could emphasize the flow process. Likewise a lesson that illustrates the process of how a user accesses QMF

FIGURE 6–9 Page Format for Process Displays

HOW WORK ORDERS ARE PROCESSED

Introduction   As the Accountant, you will be responsible for monitoring the flow of work orders. In order to understand your role, take a look at the overall work order process below.

Work Order   This diagram summarizes the work order process.
Process
Diagram

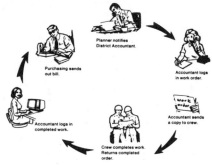

Your   Note that you will be logging the work orders in and
Role   out.

software in a mainframe environment could use overlays and arrows to illustrate terminal access to TSO then to DB2 and finally to QMF.

Process Simulations on CBT

In Chapter 3, I discussed the use of guided and unguided simulations to teach procedures related to the use of computer software or equipment involving dials and buttons that could be displayed on computer. You could take the animated process displays described above one step further and create simulations of the process. In a simulation the learner can use a program that behaves like the real process, and learn about it in an interactive way. For example, a simulated steam generator might include valves that could be manipulated and gauges that would change in response to different stages in the process. The learner would "see" the pro-

FIGURE 6–10 A Process Display for CBT Using Mainframe Authoring System

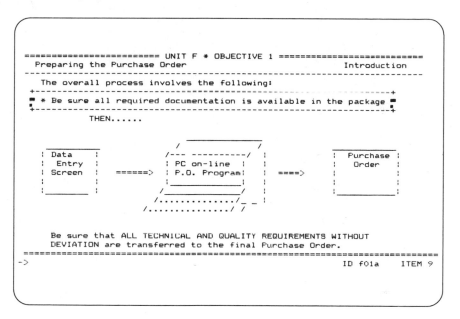

```
=========================== UNIT F * OBJECTIVE 1 ============================
  Preparing the Purchase Order                            Introduction
---------------------------------------------------------------------------
     The overall process involves the following:
  +----------------------------------------------------------------------+
  ■ * Be sure all required documentation is available in the package ■
  ■                                                                      ■
  +----------------------------------------------------------------------+
             THEN......

                            /  _____  /
      _____          /               /
    : Data     :        /--- ----------/  :            : Purchase :
    : Entry    :        : PC on-line   :  :            : Order    :
    : Screen   :  =====> : P.O. Program:  :   ====>    :          :
    :          :        :_____:  :            :          :
    :_____:          /            /   :            :_____:
                          /............./ _ _ :
                          /............../ /

      Be sure that ALL TECHNICAL AND QUALITY REQUIREMENTS WITHOUT
      DEVIATION are transferred to the final Purchase Order.
============================================================================
->                                               ID f01a    ITEM 9
```

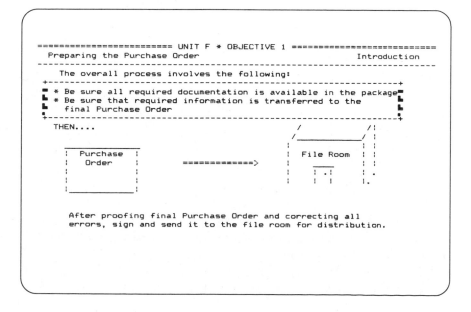

```
=========================== UNIT F * OBJECTIVE 1 ============================
  Preparing the Purchase Order                            Introduction
---------------------------------------------------------------------------
     The overall process involves the following:
  +----------------------------------------------------------------------+
  ■ * Be sure all required documentation is available in the package■
  ■ * Be sure that required information is transferred to the         ■
  ■    final Purchase Order                                           ■
  +----------------------------------------------------------------------+
     THEN....                                   /_____ /:
                                              /             / :
      _____                          :             :  :
    : Purchase     :                          : File Room   :  :
    : Order        :        ============>      :             :  :
    :              :                           :    :  .:    :  .
    :              :                           :    :  :     :  :
    :_____:                           :    :  :     :. .
                                                   : : :

      After proofing final Purchase Order and correcting all
      errors, sign and send it to the file room for distribution.
```

FIGURE 6–11 Using Animation to Illustrate a Process on Computer

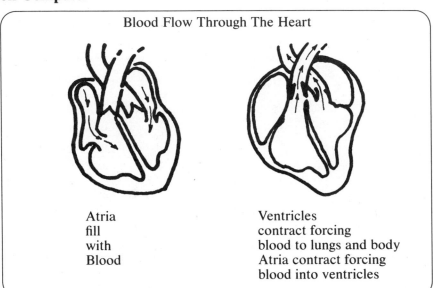

Blood Flow Through The Heart

Atria
fill
with
Blood

Ventricles
contract forcing
blood to lungs and body
Atria contract forcing
blood into ventricles

Color and Animation Would Effectively Display a Dynamic Process

cess in action and experience it more directly than through a description.

Simulations are very popular with learners, but take more time and effort to create than the more standard techniques described above. Consider developing a simulated process when process knowledge is essential to effective job performance, and when computer delivery is a more cost-effective or safe way to provide this training.

TRAINING PROCESSES: INSTRUCTIONAL TECHNIQUES FOR PRACTICE

In planning practice around processes, you need to think through your purpose in presenting the process. Sometimes you won't need to design any practice. In the lesson on how to brush your teeth, for example, the instructional outcome of the lesson is to train

FIGURE 6–12 Displaying a Software Access Process on CBT

```
QMF Overview
------------------------------------------------------------------------------

         While MVS or VM manages the whole system, two more systems handle
         communications.

         *  MVS has TSO (Time
            Sharing Options)                        .------------------------.
                                                    3 MVS (or VM)            3
         *  VM has CMS                              3------------------------.  3
            (Conversational                         3 TSO (or CMS)        3  3
            Monitor System)           .-----------.  3                    3  3
                                      3 logon .. ========>                3  3
                                      3           3  3                    3  3
                                      +-----------+  3                    3  3
                                   .------+ +------.  3                    3  3
                                   3 ::::::::::::: 3 3------------------+  3
                                   +---------------+ 3                       3
                                                    +------------------------+
         Your first step in accessing QMF will usually be to "log on" to
         TSO or CMS.
------------------------------------------------------------------------------
1.1.180           M = Menu    P = Page Back     Enter = Page Forward
```

```
QMF Overview
------------------------------------------------------------------------------

         Once you are in TSO or CMS you
         need to access QMF, which runs
         under the control of one more
         piece of software, the "Data Base
         Manager".  This is either:                .------------------------.
                                                    3 MVS (or VM)            3
                                                    3------------------------.  3
         *  DB2 (Database 2)                        3 TSO (or CMS)        3  3
                                                    3  .----------------.  3  3
            OR                        .-----------.  3  3DB2 (or SQL/DS)3  3  3
                                      3           3  3  3-------.        3  3  3
         *  SQL/DS                    3           ========> QMF   3        3  3  3
            (Structured Query         +-----------+  3  3-------+        3  3  3
            Language/Data           .------+ +------.  3  +----------------+  3  3
            System)                 3 ::::::::::::: 3 3------------------------+  3
                                    +---------------+ 3                          3
                                                    +------------------------+
------------------------------------------------------------------------------
1.1.190           M = Menu    P = Page Back     Enter = Page Forward
```

The Courseware Developers. Used with Permission.

learners correct techniques for toothbrushing. The information on the process of tooth decay was intended primarily to provide greater understanding of why toothbrushing is important. The decay process is included as a "nice-to-know" part of the lesson. No learning objective is written for the process and no practice is provided. Similarly, the lesson on the work order process was provided as background information for the accountant, to aid his understanding of the overall paper flow. Neither learning objectives nor practice were provided.

In contrast, if the work of the employee will be substantially aided by an understanding of the process, practice is warranted. Employees involved in troubleshooting either equipment or customer problems are common examples. Knowledge of how the erylitizer works is necessary for the erylitizer maintenance engineer. Programmer coding will be directly improved by an understanding of the control and flow processes of the software.

Practice should be designed to match the learning objective at the application rather than the remember level. Don't ask the engineer to list the five major stages in the operation of the erylitizer. Instead develop an exercise, like the one in Figure 6–13 that matches the objective written on page 126 which requires erylitizer problem-solving based on a description of malfunction. Similarly, suppose a customer calls in upset about an overdue notice on her bill. To respond effectively, the customer service representative must be able to apply her knowledge of the billing cycle to this particular customer's situation. Practice exercises presenting a variety of customer queries would help the representative apply her knowledge of the billing process.

Programmers taking a course on a generalized on-line coding system are presented the tree diagram shown in Figure 6–8 illustrating the processing tasks involved in an update transaction. The practice exercise shown in Figure 6–15 requires interpretation of the functions and interrelationships. This level of understanding will help the programmer when he begins coding various parts of the system. The key to the design of process exercises for employees involved in problem-solving is to collect realistic case studies of common malfunctions, customer questions, etc. that can be converted into practice exercises. As a technical expert you probably have access to a variety of these types of incidents that could be built into case-study problems for practice exercises.

FIGURE 6–13 Design Exercise at Application Rather than Remember Level

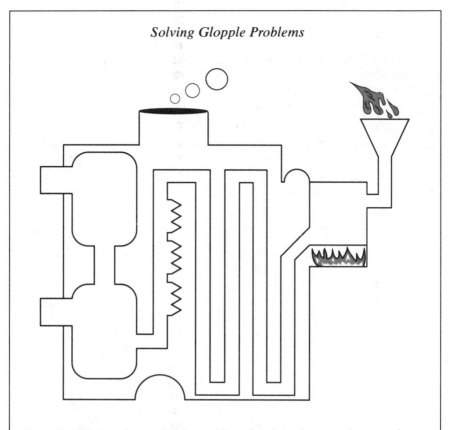

Solving Glopple Problems

Exercise: State the probable malfunction based on each scenario and describe what diagnostic steps you would take:

1. Glopples exiting from acid bath look like this: ⧗ ⧗

2. Glopples lack tensile strenth. Heat reactor warning light is on.

3. Glopples exhibit greenish hue on surface.

4. Oil pressure valve is below normal and uncharacteristic gurgling sound is noticed by operator.

FIGURE 6–14 Process Exercise Written at Application Level

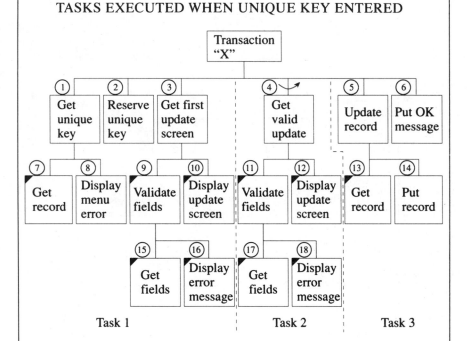

How Update Transactions Are Processed

Match the number of the box to the process described below:

TASKS EXECUTED WHEN UNIQUE KEY ENTERED

1. _____ John fills in date incorrectly and gets an error message.
2. _____ The Master file record is rewritten.
3. _____ Karen misspells the transaction on the menu.
4. _____ The Order-In-Progress Table locks the record.
5. _____ An update screen with no data is displayed.

Design of Practice on Computer

The same guidelines used for the design of process practice in the classroom apply to CBT as well. However, since the computer cannot analyze responses to open-ended questions such as "Describe what would happen if there were leakage between the right and left ventricle," more structured formats need to be designed. The matching or multiple choice format shown in Figure 6–14 would lend itself directly to CBT delivery.

Practice Using Simulations   If you are using an authoring system with simulation capabilities, some creative exercises could be designed capitalizing on those features. For example suppose you asked: "What is the likely result of leakage between the right and left ventricle?" The learner could manipulate a simulation of circulation to see what would happen. Or the simulation could be used to provide feedback by responding as would the real system.

Highly sophisticated systems with videodisk capabilities have provided realistic simulations of complex technical processes, giving learners the opportunity to troubleshoot various problems and immediately see the impact of their decisions on the system. Descriptions of these are included in *Instructional Designs for Microcomputer Courseware,* edited by Jonassen, which is referenced in the bibliography.

While these kinds of training systems are visually exciting, use care in determining how faithful your simulation must be to obtain the instructional result you need. Highly faithful simulations are expensive in terms of hardware and software development, and, except for some highly critical jobs, can be overkill. As a general rule, start out with a simpler instructional system and evaluate outcomes on job performance before investing in elaborate and expensive simulations.

Testing for Acquisition of Process Knowledge

This brings us to the question of how to evaluate that you have been successful in transmitting process knowledge to trainees. First consider your instructional objective. If the major objective is to perform a procedure and the process information is provided as background information, you need not write a learning objective or provide practice or evaluate learning.

However, if the process knowledge is critical to the procedure or is the major intended outcome of the lesson, evaluation is needed. Use formats similar to the practice exercises you have designed. If you have been training customer service representatives to solve customer billing problems based on their knowledge of the billing cycle, generate test items that provide customer questions to be resolved. While the formats should be similar to the practice exercises, vary the actual scenarios involved.

PREVIEW OF CHAPTER SEVEN

We have now reviewed how to teach four of the five major types of content in all training systems. One last type, principles, remains. Our discussion of principles will lead us into a consideration of two categories of training outcomes: near- and far-transfer. In the next chapter I will discuss the issues you need to consider when deciding how and when to teach principles as part of your instructional system. To help you in situations where you do need to train at the principle level, techniques to present and practice principles at the application level will be stressed.

The Content-Performance Matrix: Principles

	Facts	Concepts	Processes	Procedures	Principles
Apply	/////	Classify new Examples *Which file name is valid?* *A. 043MYFILE* *B. MYFILE9*	Solve A Problem Make An Inference *Customer asks about his bill. Where should you check first?*	Perform the Procedure *Log onto the Computer*	**Solve A Problem Make An Inference** ***Close this sale following the guidelines***
Remember	Remember the Facts *What is your computer password?*	Remember the Definition *Define Valid File Name*	Remember the Stages *Describe How Work Orders Are Processed*	Remember the Steps *List the Steps to Log onto the Computer*	**Remember the Guidelines** ***List the rules for closing a sale***

Far-Transfer Training: How to Teach Principles

CHAPTER SUMMARY

- Your major training goals can be classified as either near- or far-transfer. Near-transfer training is procedural, involving specific steps to be followed more or less the same way each time. Far-transfer training involves the translation of guidelines or principles into the steps that best fit a given work situation which will vary each time.

- While near-transfer tasks are easier to train, with greater probability of success, the employee is limited to performing the tasks as taught. Far-transfer tasks are more difficult to train and the probability of successful outcomes is lower. But once the guidelines are acquired, the employee is able to apply the skills to a variety of job-related contexts.

- Identifying the principles that best support optimal job performance is one of the major challenges of far-transfer training. You can identify valid principles through relevant scientific sources or by abstracting guidelines from a comparison of master and average performances. Two ways to collect data for abstracting principles are analysis of multiple job performance examples and use of critical incidents to generate a range of responses from experts.

- Like the other types of content, principles should be trained at the application level of performance. This means that trainees must practice successful implementation of guidelines in a variety of job-related situations often presented as case studies.

• To teach principles, you need to provide the relevant guidelines. Varied context examples illustrate successful application of the principles to diverse situations. Non-examples can be provided to illustrate the difference between successful and unsuccessful application of principles.

• Analogies are an especially powerful instructional method in the training of principles. To work, the analogy must be familiar to the learners. Its critical elements must link meaningfully to the principle. Analogies are most effective when the guidelines taught are unfamiliar to the target audience.

• Practice of principles is most effective in two stages. First, require the learner to identify appropriate and inappropriate implementations of the guidelines from examples you provide. Second, ask the learner to apply the principles to a variety of job-related situations.

• Far-transfer training that involves application of social skills, such as supervisory or sales training, is best taught in a classroom setting where video scenarios and role-playing can provide realistic examples and practice with feedback. Some of the basic social-skill information can be provided beforehand on computer to save classroom time.

• Far-transfer training delivered on computer may be difficult to practice, due to structured response formats imposed by CBT. Because it is not possible to evaluate open-ended responses, you may be constrained when designing practice for application of principles for computer delivery. This limitation can be overcome if the principles to be trained and the background of the trainees are suitable.

• Practice of some principles at the application level can be accomplished via CBT simulations. A simulation is a scaled-down enactment of a real-world situation. In a simulation, the trainee can manipulate various aspects of a "microworld" and see the effects. Simulations are especially useful when the real setting is dangerous or expensive, or occurs over long time periods, but they are time-consuming to construct. Evaluate the value of the simulation to your training goal in terms of cost-benefit tradeoffs.

• Testing the acquisition of principles is challenging, due to the judgment required by instructors. Behavioral checklists and instructor/rater training should be provided to make the evaluations as consistent as possible.

In Chapter 3, I described how to train procedures, one of the most common target skills of many technical training programs. Procedures consist of a series of steps which are performed more or less the same way each time the task is done. Whereas in linear procedures the steps typically follow a similar sequence, in branched procedures more than one sequence of steps may be followed. For example, logging onto the computer is a linear procedure, while assigning a code to indicate customer credit status is a branched procedure.

There are however, some training goals that are not procedural in nature. There are no exact steps that can be specified because the situation or context in which the task takes place will be different each time. For example, suppose you were teaching first-line supervisors how to handle an employee who approached them with a personal problem such as an alcoholic spouse. Or imagine training technical experts how to be effective classroom instructors. In both situations training can provide guidelines, but learners will need to use judgment in applying the guidelines to fit the circumstances.

This chapter will begin with a discussion of the differences between near-transfer (procedural) and far-transfer (principle-based) training. I will then describe how to define the principles for far-transfer training, since this is a more difficult task than defining the steps of near-transfer training. The next part of the chapter will discuss how to train principles with relevant examples for classroom and computer media. Finally, ways to evaluate successful acquisition of principles will be described.

FIGURE 7–1 **Near- and Far-Transfer Training**

Near	Far
Steps Performed Same Way Each Time	**Guidelines Implemented Differently Each Time**
How to log onto the computer	How to respond to an employee with personal problems
STEPS	GUIDELINES
step 1 xxxxxxxxxx	guideline 1 xxxxxxxxxxxxxxx
step 2 xxxxxxxxxx	guideline 2 xxxxxxxxxxxxxxx
step 3 xxxxxxxxxx	guideline 3 xxxxxxxxxxxxxxx

NEAR- AND FAR-TRANSFER TRAINING

As illustrated in Figure 7–1, the distinction between step-by-step training and training that involves application of more general guidelines can be summarized in the concepts of *near-* and *far-transfer* training outcomes. Near-transfer training involves the teaching of tasks which are procedural in nature. That is, you can show the employee the exact steps he should take to achieve the work goal. In near-transfer training the skills are applied the same way each time the task is undertaken; logging onto the computer is an example. By contrast, far-transfer tasks are performed under circumstances that change each time. Since the actual steps must be adapted to fit each situation and will be different every time, learners are trained to implement the basic principles or guidelines.

Distinguishing Between Near- and Far-Transfer Training

Most training programs involve a combination of near- and far-transfer tasks, but one of the two types usually predominates. Because the teaching techniques differ, you need to decide whether your goals call for near- or far-transfer training. Ask yourself if your instructional goal requires your trainees to follow a prescribed set of steps in a relatively consistent environment. Or will the task circumstances be changing sufficiently each time that you need to train them to effectively apply guidelines? In most organizations far-transfer training deals either with application of social skills or with unique problem resolution. Social tasks include training in effective supervision, customer service, and sales techniques. Far-transfer training involving problem-solving of a non-routine nature includes such tasks as advanced troubleshooting for equipment maintenance, installing a quality management system into a department, and strategic business planning. As a general rule, there is a positive relationship between the level of employee and the amount of far-transfer work she is assigned — i.e. high-level employees tend to be assigned a greater proportion of far-transfer tasks.

There are advantages and disadvantages to both types of training. Near-transfer tasks are easier to train and give you a good chance of getting the specified result you want if you follow the appropriate teaching steps. On the other hand, while the employee will be well equipped to perform the tasks as you trained them, if task-related circumstances change they will not be prepared to adapt.

By contrast, far-transfer tasks are more challenging to instruct. Because the employee will have to adapt the guidelines to fit the various situations in which they will be applied, the likelihood of success is less than with near-transfer tasks. On the other hand, once the skills are acquired, the employee is more versatile because he can use judgment to make adjustments to the performance of the task as circumstances dictate.

Sometimes you may have to make a decision on whether to train at a near- or far-transfer level. Teaching electronic troubleshooting is one example. You may want entry-level employees to quickly learn to perform routine troubleshooting procedures that will resolve 75% of the common problems. They will know what signs to look for and what components to replace based on those signs with little understanding of why. As they won't need much knowledge of electrical theory, their training will be designed around branched procedural content. In contrast, you may also need more advanced employees who can form hypotheses and resolve problems not encountered before. This requires a greater depth of knowledge to support the application of principles to various unpredictable situations. Their training will be principle-based.

CHECK YOUR UNDERSTANDING

To be sure you can distinguish between near- and far-transfer tasks, try the short exercise on page 247

Far-Transfer Training and Principles

If you are going to be training far-transfer tasks, you will be working with principles which underlie or make up the guidelines to be trained. A principle is a cause-and-effect relationship that results in a predictable outcome. The most valid principles are based on scientific research from the physical, biological, or social sciences. For example, "Greater productivity results when employees are given specific challenging assignments accompanied by feedback and appropriate consequences" is a cause-and-effect statement which has been verified by research. This principle can form the basis of guidelines for management training sessions where supervisors and managers learn to construct specific and challenging assignments for their subordinates. What constitutes a specific and challenging assignment varies from task to task and from employee to employee. Such guidelines cannot be taught as procedures.

Identifying the Principles You Need

One of the more critical and challenging aspects of far-transfer training is identifying the principles that best support your training goal. A valid principle is one that, when applied, yields the predicted or desired result. Your goal might be to teach managers ways to increase employee productivity, or to teach sales staff how best to close a sale. How do you identify the principles that will form the core of your training?

If you are a technical expert developing procedural training, it is not too difficult for you to identify the steps you typically follow to complete the task. But you cannot do this in far-transfer training. That's because, even if you're an expert performer, your way is not the only path to success. In fact, your way may not work for other employees. In far-transfer training, you will have to do additional research to identify the appropriate guidelines to be trained. I will briefly describe some techniques here. The books

FIGURE 7–2 How to Identify the Principles You Need

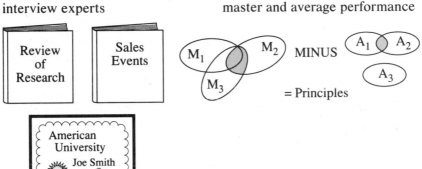

cited under needs assessment and task analysis in the bibliography are recommended for more detailed information.

Figure 7–2 summarizes two approaches you can use to define the guidelines you need: drawing on scientific research, and abstracting commonalities from multiple effective performances and comparing them to ineffective performances. A combination of both techniques will give you the best data from which to derive the principles most applicable to the setting in question.

Drawing on Scientific Research In the sciences you can find research that provides guidelines applicable to various business problems. For example, from the social sciences, studies on how to best obtain maximum employee productivity indicate the following guidelines:

- provide specific and challenging work assignments
- monitor and provide feedback on the quantity and quality of work
- provide positive consequences for desired outcomes

In environments where work assignments are vague or undemanding, where the results of the work are never known, or where incentives have nothing to do with work results, productivity will decline. These guidelines could provide you with the basis for part of a management/supervisory training program.

If you are not an expert in the area to be trained, you might look for a recognized expert who could help you identify the most relevant research guidelines. Your local university or professional society might be a resource for individuals with expertise in a particular field. If you are a technical expert you may already be familiar with the key principles of your field. You may need only to identify those that best relate to your desired training goals.

A second approach is to abstract the basic principles or guidelines by analyzing the actions of master, contrasted to average, performers. Techniques for gathering this data include direct performance observations and critical-incident research.

Observing Performance

Your first step will be to identify employees whose work has been independently validated as superior and compare it with the performance of those whose work is average or below. Independent validation means you have an objective measure of performance — not just someone's opinion. Sales volume is a good indicator of effective marketing performance. Instructor rating sheets would provide good validation of instructors who are perceived as effective by their students. Student achievement results would be a valid indicator of instructional effectiveness.

It is critical to observe several master performers in order not to consider a top performer's specific techniques as an important feature. You need to look at commonalities among the top performers *not shared* by less proficient employees. For example, an evaluation of several highly rated instructors showed some to be dynamic and energetic, while others were quieter in their presentation. Their surface characteristics were quite different. What turned out to be a critical underlying factor of instructor success was the individual's ability to sustain attention in a supportive manner. Some instructors did this with humor, some with animated presentations, and others with interrogative teaching techniques that kept the participants actively involved.

Collecting Critical Incidents

You may be in a situation where it is not practical or possible to observe actual job performance. An alternative technique for abstracting elements of master performance involves interviewing relevant sources for incidents that characterize effective job actions. You can collect this type of data via individual interviews, structured group discussions, or questionnaires.

What to Ask   You might begin with general questions. For example: "Think of the top sales performers in your district. What are some of the things they do that make them successful? Describe actual situations . . . Now think about your less effective employees. What things do they omit? Describe some actions they take that are ineffective."

Based on responses to these general questions, you might begin to focus in on more specific situations which could serve as critical incidents. A critical incident is a job situation which, if handled effectively or ineffectively, has a major impact on the outcome of the task. Here are two examples of critical incidents.

1. After the account representative presents the major features and benefits of the new personnel software system to the client, the data-processing manager raises an objection about interfaces with his existing systems. How should the account representative respond?

2. Mark is teaching a public course on database software. The course uses SQL as the major example. One of the students raises her hand and says "All your examples use SQL — but that's not the software used at my company. I don't think this course is going to be of any use to me!" What should Mark say to handle the comment effectively?

Collect a variety of answers to such critical incidents from knowledgeable sources and look for commonalities in the patterns of answers. Abstract the relevant guidelines from these responses.

Whom to Ask   It will be important that you collect critical incidents from respondents who are knowledgeable. One obvious choice is experienced managers who have supervised and coached a variety of workers. Or interview top and average performers asking them What-would-you-do-if questions based on the critical incidents. Consider gathering data from the customer or consumer of the products or services of the job to be trained. As customers might not be familiar enough with the job to describe how to respond to the situations, you might develop multiple-choice options and ask them to indicate their preference. An example is illustrated

FIGURE 7–3 **Abstracting Relevant Guidelines from Customer Preferences**

Circle all responses that would be acceptable to you:

When checking out from your hotel you notice you are charged for credit card calls made from your room. You were unaware of additional charges and ask the check-out agent about it. The agent responds:

a. All hotels in this state charge a connect fee for credit calls.
b. Didn't you see the notice in your room?
c. You will need to speak to the manager.
d. I'll subtract the charges from your bill.
e. It's hotel policy to treat those calls like a local call.

in Figure 7–3. As with the observations, be sure to collect data from several sources and to abstract commonalities.

Combining Research Approaches   In general, it's a good idea to use a combination of research techniques, including literature reviews or interviews of recognized experts, observations of independently validated top performers and management interviews. This will help you see how well the research data fit the environment of the group to be trained. As a secondary benefit, the direct involvement of the target group will promote greater buy-in to the resulting training.

Learning Principles at the Remember and Application Levels

As we have seen in Chapters 3–6, all the types of content except facts can be processed at the remember and the application levels. The need to train at the application level has been emphasized throughout. Principles are no different. At the remember level the employee can recall or recognize the principle. For example, the management trainee can say, "Set specific and challenging goals for maximum productivity," but this does not mean that he will be able to actually implement the principle when making a work assignment. At the application level, the trainee takes action which is congruent with the guidelines presented. He must learn to proceduralize the principle generating the steps most appropriate to the current situation being faced. Thus the management trainee

FIGURE 7–4 Translating Principles Into Procedures

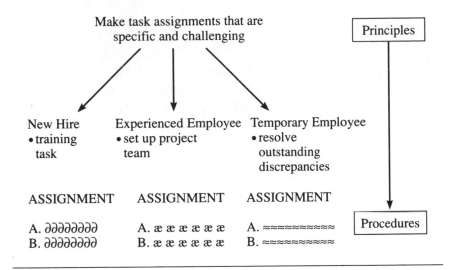

GENERAL GUIDELINES

Make task assignments that are
specific and challenging

Principles

New Hire
• training
  task

Experienced Employee
• set up project
  team

Temporary Employee
• resolve
  outstanding
  discrepancies

ASSIGNMENT   ASSIGNMENT   ASSIGNMENT

A. ∂∂∂∂∂∂∂   A. æ æ æ æ æ æ   A. ≈≈≈≈≈≈≈≈≈   Procedures
B. ∂∂∂∂∂∂∂   B. æ æ æ æ æ æ   B. ≈≈≈≈≈≈≈≈≈

could make up different task assignments for specific employees or for various work goals, all of which followed the guideline of being specific and challenging.

Writing Principle Learning Objectives at the Application Level

Lesson Objectives   If your lesson tasks are far-transfer, your main lesson objective should be written at the "application-of-a-principle" level. Instead of a remember-level objective such as "List the five guidelines for effective sale closure," an objective at the application level would read: "You will be given a specific product, product catalog, and customer description. You will role-play closing the sale, using the five guidelines for effective closures." If you were designing training to teach technical instructors effective classroom skills, your objective might read: "You will present a five-minute lesson from your technical course. Your lesson must include six questions targeted in three different ways. You must apply the 3R response techniques to the answers you receive." Notice that principle-based learning objectives ask the trainee to respond to the job-relevant situation by appropriately applying the guidelines.

Supporting Objectives   In addition to your main lesson objective that requires the learner to apply principles to the job task, some supporting objectives are often necessary in far-transfer training. In our sales training course it would be helpful to ask learners to identify appropriate and inappropriate applications of the principles before trying them out themselves. Thus a supporting objective might state: "You will watch ten videotaped sales closures. For each you will decide if the guidelines were applied effectively and state what improvements if any are needed." The instructor training lesson might focus on identification of different question types and responses with an objective that asked learners to classify a series of sample instructor-student exchanges. Once you have identified a valid set of principles and written your learning objectives, your next challenge will be to develop training that enables employees to apply them to the diverse changing situations they will face.

TRAINING TECHNIQUES FOR FAR-TRANSFER TRAINING

In general the strategy for teaching procedures is to provide the steps and a demonstration accompanied by guided practice until the employee performs the procedure confidently. In far-transfer training the approach will be different. After the guidelines are presented, a series of varied context examples should be provided which illustrate how the guidelines can be applied in diverse circumstances. Such examples show how the application of the guidelines will look in the alternative situations the employee is likely to encounter. In addition, some non-examples of applying guidelines are recommended. At this point practice should require the trainee to observe sample tasks and identify which ones effectively implement the guidelines. Discussion of ways to improve the ineffective examples should be designed into the exercise. Finally, the trainee must practice applying the guidelines to a series of varied context situation exercises usually presented in the form of case studies. The next section will take a more detailed look at how to train principles. As with all the five content types, training techniques are of two major types: information displays and practice exercises.

Training Principles: Informational Instructional Techniques

State the Principle   When teaching principles, first provide a statement of the principle itself, followed by the guidelines which flow from it. An elaboration of the rationale for the principle can also be included. If you were teaching supervisors how to deal with an employee with personal problems, the general principle to be presented is: "You want to maintain a constructive relationship with the employee and you are not legally qualified to give professional advice on personal problems." Guidelines that follow include:

1. After the employee has presented the problem, respond with paraphrasing and empathy so the employee knows you heard her
2. Tell the employee you are not qualified to give advice on these matters
3. Refer the employee to the appropriate company or community resource for professional help
4. Follow up by asking whether help was obtained and how things are going.

Provide Varied Context Examples   After providing a statement or description of the principle and guidelines to follow, a series of varied context examples is needed to illustrate the application of the principle in typical work-related situations. Our supervisory training program might include several videotaped examples. One might show a supervisor responding to an employee claiming her spouse had abused her. Another might show a supervisor responding to an employee asking for help in dealing with a child on drugs. A third might begin with a supervisor discussing a performance problem with an employee. When the employee uses his recent divorce as an excuse for the performance problem, the supervisor must call on the employee problem guidelines and recommend help. Then the supervisor must continue to address the performance problem. Note the various contexts and increasing complexity of examples.

Provide Varied Context Non-examples   After showing a variety of situations in which the guidelines are effectively applied, you might present some non-examples. It will be important to build in cues that show how the non-examples ignore the guidelines. In our supervisory training program, a non-example on video might show a supervisor describing his experiences in his own divorce or discuss what his best friend John did to resolve an alcohol problem. The instruction would need to show that, while the supervisor is attempting to be supportive, he or she is not qualified to give this type of assistance and could be held legally liable, and that the employee is entitled to the most competent professional resources available. For these reasons the actions ignore the guidelines.

Analogies: A Key Information Display

After a statement of the principle and guidelines accompanied by varied context examples and non-examples, an analogy is a very efficient technique for presenting principles. Analogies are efficient because they call on existing knowledge to explain a new relationship. For adding fractions, the slice-of-pie analogy is commonly used to show how two-fourths add up to a half. For teaching fundamentals of voltage and resistance, an analogy of water moved by various sized pumps through pipes of different diameters is often used.

In a quality-improvement course, the Taguchi principle of reduction of variation in critical product features around a specified value is compared to the "with-in specification" definition of quality prevalent in U.S. manufacturing. A target practice analogy illustrated in Figure 7–5 is used. The trainees are asked which of two targets would be better to improve shooting accuracy: target A with circular bands only, or target B with a black circle around the center. Most agree that if the goal is to maximize shooting accuracy the cued target would result in better performance. This analogy is used to compare the Taguchi quality principle where greater accuracy hitting a target value (less variation around the target value) will result in greater overall product quality than a with-in specification goal that accepts any values within the tolerance ranges. The cued target is then related to the distribution of variation around the target value.

Many introductory computer courses have drawn on the analogy between typical office concepts, such as file folders, in-and-out baskets and filing cabinets, and computer concepts including records, files, and temporary and permanent memory storage.

While analogies are a very effective way to teach principles, coming up with the right analogy is often very difficult. First, the

FIGURE 7–5 **The Target Analogy for Taguchi Quality Principles**

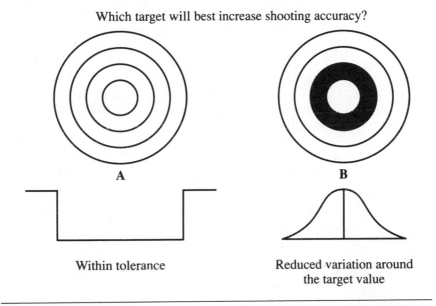

Which target will best increase shooting accuracy?

A

B

Within tolerance

Reduced variation around
the target value

basis for the analogy must be known already to the trainee. Second, the critical features of the analogy must map functionally onto the new knowledge to be taught. If you are presenting a complicated analogy it will be important to point out how the elements of the analogy map onto the new knowledge.

Formats for Training Manuals

We have seen that, in the teaching of principles, a statement of the principles and guidelines accompanied by varied context examples and non-examples make up the major informational displays. In addition, the use of an analogy is recommended when possible. Figures 7–6 through 7–9 illustrate three principle lessons designed for classroom instruction. Figure 7–6 is from a lesson for engineers to teach them how to write process specifications to be used by operators in a major semiconductor company. This page is teaching the guideline "Write specific and complete instructions." In this lesson three sets of paired examples and non-examples were used to provide immediate contrast. Note that a brief statement of the rule appears left-justified at the top. The introduction provides a statement of benefits and the definition reinforces the key features of the guideline.

FIGURE 7–6 Sample Principle Lesson for Workbook

WRITE SPECIFIC AND COMPLETE INSTRUCTIONS

Introduction	Specific and complete instructions are accurate and free from any uncertainty. They state "who" does "what" and "when".
Guideline	Write instructions that have no uncertainty. Be specific and complete. Instructions that do not specifically state who carries out the action are done by the operator. Be sure that checklists and log sheets include all headings for data that needs to be recorded.
Example	FMAs will wipe all utility piping and exterior surfaces within reach once each Monday on Shift 5 using clean room towels.
Non-example	Wipe all utility piping and exterior surfaces within reach with clean room towels.
Example	Clean all surfaces in work area with foam wipes and I.P.A. at shift start and after each run to remove all gold flakes.
Non-example	Cleaning of the area periodically is required to maintain control of the gold flakes.
Example	Record date, time, your initials, bank and tube number, and number of wafers in the log sheet.
	Record the ion gauge pressure at the beginning of the deposition cycle under the "Dep P" heading.
	Record the number of wafers out and the final thickness (TOX) in the log sheet.
	If the final thickness is not within the range listed in section 2.2 circle the out of range reading on the log sheet and hold the lot for Engineering Disposition.
Non-example	Fill out the log sheet. Hold the lot for Engineering if out of spec.

Used with permission Intel Corp.

FIGURE 7–7 Sample Principle Lesson for Workbook

PRINCIPLES OF EFFECTIVE INSTRUCTION:
ACCOUNTABILITY

Introduction	In addition to logical organization of topics that include planned active involvement on the part of your learners, you will want to build accountability into your course for maximum effectiveness.
Principle 4 Accountability	Make Training Accountable • Instructors are accountable to provide learners with validated training materials and experiences • Learners are accountable to invest effort needed to achieve objectives
Accountability and Effort	Rescarch shows that if individuals are held accountable for their performance they will invest greater effort to achieve specified goals.
Example: Instructor Training	The instructional presentations skills class requires trainees to individually make a 20 minute presentation while they are videotaped. Instructors use checklists to evaluate the results and give feedback to each person.
Nonexample: COBOL	Lois is planning a course on Cobol. She explains the coding and gives several examples. Then she assigns a project to be completed by groups of four students. At no point are individual skills assessed. By not testing individually, there is no documentation of individual achievement of objectives. Often a class will seem to be going generally well. However, nearly always there are one or two learners who are not achieving objectives and either should not be in the class or need extra help. By not measuring individual performance, the instructor will not be able to identify these learners.

FIGURE 7–8 Illustration to Accompany Sample Principle Workbook Lesson

Principles of Effective, Efficient Instruction

4. Make training accountable!
   (competency-based training).
   a. The course is valid — it teaches what it says it teaches.

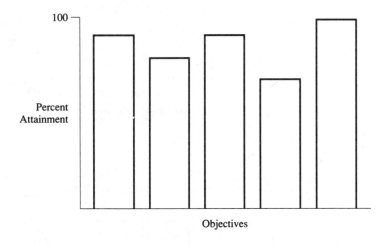

b. The learners are measured for achievement of objectives.

Figures 7–7 and 7–8 present one of four principles of effective instruction from a lesson that introduces my Instructional Development Workshop. A summary of the principle is included in the left-justified title and stated in the section labeled "Principle 4 Accountability." In this example, the introduction provides a transition from the prior three principles to the fourth. The non-example is made salient by an explanation that accountability means collecting individual products demonstrating achievement of objectives. A visual illustration shown in Figure 7–8 is used to reinforce the dual nature of accountability.

None of these examples made use of an analogy. Figure 7–9 shows a part of a lesson on how a fluid connection between engines and automatic transmissions transmits and increases torque. A fan analogy is used to depict how the fluid transmits torque between the engine and torque converter. For presenting analogies, a visual illustration is especially helpful.

FIGURE 7–9 Use of an Analogy to Illustrate Principles of System Development

FLUID COUPLING BETWEEN ENGINE AND TORQUE CONVERTER

Introduction — As we have seen, the torque converter can be physically connected to the engine when the clutch is engaged. However, maximum torque increase is gained when the engine and torque converter are connected through the hydraulic fluid.

How It Works — When the engine rotates the input shaft and the clutch is disengaged, the hydraulic fluid flows from the impeller to the turbine. When thrown back onto the impeller, its rotation is increased more, thus increasing overall torque.

Fan Analogy — The fluid coupling between engine and torque converter is a bit like the impact of two fans on each other. Fan 1 driven by the engine blows air at a high speed onto Fan 2, which in turn increases the speed of Fan 1. Increased blade turning of Fan 1 results from the additional air generated from Fan 2.

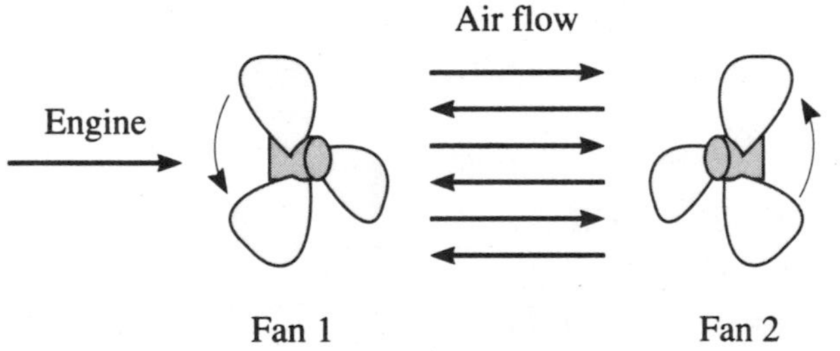

Air flow

Engine

Fan 1   Fan 2

Formats for Computer-Based Training

The informational displays needed to communicate principles effectively are the same for CBT as for workbooks. The instruction needs to provide a statement of the principle, along with guidelines and a series of varied context examples and non-examples. Again analogies reinforced with visual illustrations are very effective and efficient instructional tools.

The CBT screens illustrated in Figures 7–10A through 7–10D show the use of overlays to present examples and non-examples of

FIGURE 7–10 Sample Principle Lesson from CBT

CBT Development Guidelines   Lesson 2 — page 3 of 9

   Because the screen is small, follow these guidelines to make
   your CBT text more readable: Use:

   • the ACTIVE VOICE
   • the SECOND PERSON
   • SHORT words and sentences

   PF 1 = BACK   PF 2 = HELP   PF 3 = MENU   PF 4 = QUIT

A.   State the Guidelines

CBT Development Guidelines   Lesson 2 — page 4 of 9

ACTIVE VOICE

THIS: Depress the shift enter key to insert a page break		
NOT THIS: To insert a page break the shift enter key is depressed		

   PF 1 = BACK   PF 2 HELP   PF 3 = MENU   PF 4 = QUIT

B.   Provide Examples/Non-examples

CBT Development Guidelines   Lesson 2 — page 5 of 9

SECOND PERSON

ACTIVE VOICE THIS: Depress the shift enter key to insert a page break	THIS: If you are new to the program, start with Option A.	
NOT THIS: To insert a page break the shift enter key is depressed	NOT THIS: If the user is new to the program, start with Option A	

PF 1 = BACK   PF 2 = HELP   PF 3 = MENU   PF 4 = QUIT

C.   Use Overlay to Provide Examples/Non-examples

CBT Development Guidelines   Lesson 2 — page 6 of 9

SHORT WORDS, SENTENCES

ACTIVE VOICE	SECOND PERSON	
THIS: Depress the shift enter key to insert a page break	THIS: If you are new to the program, start with Option A.	THIS: Be sure the computer is plugged in before turning on
NOT THIS: To insert a page break the shift enter key is depressed	NOT THIS: If the user is new to the program, start with Option A	NOT THIS: One must check the power source prior to activation of the...

PF 1 = BACK   PF 2 = HELP   PF 3 = MENU   PF 4 = QUIT

D.   Use Overlay to Provide Examples/Non-examples

some basic writing rules applied to writing computer lessons. Because the target audience is assumed to be familiar with the basic concepts behind the rules, no analogy is required.

Design of Practice Exercises for Classroom Training of Principles

As with the other types of content, it is important to design practice that will require your learners to apply the principles, not just recall them. Far-transfer training usually benefits from at least two practice sessions. The first one encourages the learner to evaluate sample performances and determine their effectiveness. The next requires the learner to apply the principles. For the final practice you will need to design several scenarios that will require the trainees to resolve problems by using the guidelines taught. The scenarios should, like the examples, be from various contexts. In our supervisory skills training session, scenarios of employees approaching their supervisor with personal problems of various types could be designed and the trainees asked to role-play their responses. The employee dialogue could be written out in the training manual or, for maximum realism, they could be videotaped.

As mentioned before, much principle-based training in areas such as sales and supervisor management involves application of social skills. The most appropriate practice mode for social skills is role play with a video recording for feedback. Therefore, this type of training is most appropriate for classroom delivery. However, as we will see below, the classroom training time can be reduced by providing some of the training on computer. The difficult aspect of this training is the judgment required by the instructor. Because there is no single set of "correct" answers, the instructor has to use judgment to determine how effectively the guidelines were translated into specific action steps for each scenario.

A sample workbook exercise from the writing process specifications course is illustrated in Figure 7–11. The trainee is provided with some specifications which violate the guidelines and asked to rewrite them. In my Instructional Development Workshop, after an introduction to the four principles of effective instruction, the first exercise shown in Figure 7–12 presents a brief scenario and asks the trainee to determine which principles have been applied. A later exercise will require the learners to apply the principles to their own training design. In a management training course, the principle being trained is: "Specific challenging assignments with

FIGURE 7–11 **Sample Principle Practice for Workbook**

Write Specific and Complete Instructions — Practice

Below are several portions of specifications. Rewrite each one applying the guidelines of specific and complete instructions.

1. Re-surfscan each wafer and calculate deltas and averages for each group.

2. Learn the format number from Process Engineering.

3. Clean vacuum wands.

4. Change the acid according to acid change schedule.

FIGURE 7–12 **Sample Principle Practice for Workbook**

Applying Principles of Effective Instruction — Practice 1

For each scenario described below, identify which principles have been violated and describe what the instructor could do to use the principles which were ignored.

1. Marsha is scheduled to teach a one-hour class on confined space monitoring. In order to get in all the material, she has to lecture very quickly for the entire hour. At the end of the hour, Marsha tells the learners to call her if they have any problems when they try the procedure.

2. JoAnne is preparing to teach new-hire trainees the procedure for processing an unresolved billing inquiry. As she plans her lesson, she meets with the current floor supervisors to be sure that her lesson reflects the way the procedure is being done. After a demonstration, she gives a case study to groups of four. The whole class discussed each case study at the end of the session.

regular feedback are better than vague easy goals." In the final exercise, trainees are provided with case studies that include descriptions of quarterly goals and background information on their staff. They are then asked to design weekly assignments for each employee. Designing task assignments for employees of different capabilities, motivation, and experience provides varied context practice opportunities for the trainees. After the trainees write out task assignments, group discussion is used to emphasize the good points and the suggested improvements for each.

The key to effective exercises is to collect realistic job problems that would require the employee to apply the guidelines to resolve them. The range of problems should vary across a number of situations the employee might encounter. As a technical expert, you will probably have access to various situations that could be adapted to serve the purpose. Otherwise, draw on the observations or critical incidents you encounter during your research to define the appropriate principles.

Designing Practice for Computer-Based Training

Because CBT requires a structured response, and appropriate responses in applying guidelines can vary, you might be somewhat limited in designing practice for applying principles on the computer. If you were instructing sales trainees on techniques to close the sale, including what signals to identify in the customer and what response to make both verbally and with body language, you could probably not provide the entire training needed on the computer. In fact, social-skills training usually requires some classroom sessions. Still classroom time can be substantially reduced by providing some of the up-front skills on the computer. The computer can effectively teach the trainee to identify the verbal signals that indicate a customer's willingness to close the sale, by using simple graphics and written dialogue. It could also initiate training on what kinds of verbal responses the sales representative should make. For the new sales person, classroom training would be needed to allow the trainee to role-play various scenarios involving closing of sales and get feedback from the instructor.

Figures 7–13 and 7–14 show practice exercises designed for the CBT lesson on writing effective text for CBT. The first exercise asks the trainee to identify the most effective applications of the principles to a series of brief written samples. Ideally, the trainee

FIGURE 7–13 **Sample Principle Practice from CBT**

CBT Development Guidelines   Lesson 2 — page 7 of 9

Which of the following sentences best applies the CBT text
guidelines of active voice, second person, simple sentences?
Choose A, B or C: _____

A. When the employee returns to work, the supervisor must sign
    the 18-60 form.
B. When asking for additional leave, get your supervisor to sign
    the approval form (3-13).
C. When terminating the shift rotation cycle all processing books
    must be monitored to insure accurate signoffs.

PF 1 = BACK   PF 2 = HELP   PF 3 = MENU   PF 4 = QUIT

should then write out some sample text applying the guidelines.
Since the computer could not judge free-form text, a structured
approach is used whereby a sentence is rewritten by a sequential
selection of various choices to replace target words in the sentence. Would this technique result in better writing skills or would
actual writing practice be required? The answer really depends on
the target audience. If the learners already had some experience
writing and were familiar with the basic concepts in other settings,
chances are this training would be sufficient. Novice writers would
probably require greater instructional support than the computer
would allow. This type of CBT exercise would greatly reduce classroom time if classroom follow-up writing practice was required.

Designing Computer Simulations for Practice of Principles

We have described computer simulations to support learning of
procedures and processes. Simulations can also be used in training
of principles. A simulation is a scaled-down enactment of reality in
which the components will act in accordance with the principles.
Simulating scientific and mathematical principles works well. For
example, in a chemistry simulation the trainee can "add" via key-
presses "drops" of acid into a chemical solution graphically displayed on the screen. As the acid is added, a thermometer, a pH

FIGURE 7–14 **Sample Principle Practice from CBT**

CBT Development Guidelines   Lesson 2 — page 7 of 9

The sentence below violates the effective writing guidelines of active voice, second person, and simple sentence. You will rewrite the sentence by choosing the best phrase to replace the underlined words:

The most efficacious blend of quality and productivity can be discovered when <u>one routinely uses control charts</u>.

    a.   the supervisor uses control charts daily
    b.   you use control charts daily

PF 1 = BACK   PF 2 = HELP   PF 3 = MENU   PF 4 = QUIT

CBT Development Guidelines   Lesson 2 — page 8 of 9

The sentence below violates the effective writing guidelines of active voice, second person, and simple sentence. You will rewrite the sentence by choosing the best phrase to replace the underlined words:

If you use control charts daily, the <u>most efficacious blend</u> of quality and productivity can be discovered.

    a.   beneficial balance
    b.   best mix
    c.   optimal proportion

PF 1 = BACK   PF 2 = HELP   PF 3 = MENU   PF 4 = QUIT

indicator, and the solution's color dynamically change on the screen. The learner can conduct a number of experiments without going near the laboratory.

Simulations are useful for practice applying principles in situations that are dangerous, rare, expensive, time-consuming, or otherwise unfeasible in the normal training setting. Figure 7–15 shows a statistical process-control simulation designed for a process engineer in a manufacturing facility.

While simulations are highly motivating and effective, they are usually time-consuming and complex to construct, and typically need to be built in a lower-level language rather than an authoring system. High-resolution graphics are often required. They work best when there is a clear rule-driven set of relationships so that various states in the microworld can be reliably predicted. As mentioned before, weigh the benefits derived from a computer simulation against the time and effort involved in creating it.

FIGURE 7–15 **Sample Principle Simulation Practice From CBT**

Principles of Statistical Quality Control   Simulation

Now that you have seen how to manage the quality process using control charts, let's apply the principle to a small process. Each time you press enter, a data point will appear on the control chart. You can take any of the actions listed below at any time and see the effect on the process.

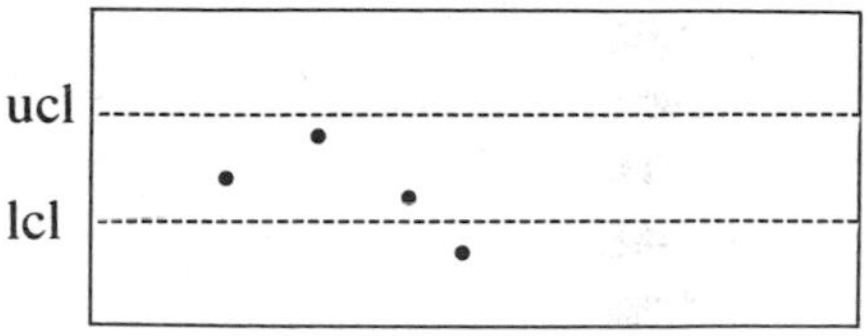

ucl

lcl

A.   Recalibrate micrometer
B.   Check input dimensions
C.   Realign die process
D.   Change vacuum pressure
ACTION DESIRED: _____

PF 1 = BACK   PF 2 = HELP   PF 3 = MENU   PF 4 = QUIT

FIGURE 7–16 Checklist Used to Evaluate Application of Presentation Skills Guidelines by New Instructors

Delivery Techniques Checklist

Delivery Techniques	Good	Work On	Comments
USE OF NOTES • notes not read • order of notes maintained • notes personalized • timelines maintained			
USE OF OHP • image in focus • size maximum • alignment square • no shoulder block • cueing techniques used • information added • sequencing logical • pacing appropriate			
APPEARANCE • formal business dress • no distractions in attire			
FACIAL EXPRESSION • smiling • animated			
EYE CONTACT • random • 3–5 seconds • back and sides covered			
GESTURES • natural and animated • emphasize points • no distractions • moves around room			
VOICE • audible • clear • vocal interest • no distractions			

Evaluating Acquisition of Principles

Evaluating the successful acquisition of principles is difficult because, as discussed above, there is no single set of "correct" answers. A range of responses that acceptably incorporate the guidelines must be identified. Test items should be similar to those provided during practice sessions. In general they should include various problems or scenarios that call for the application of the target principles.

To help instructors score such tests consistently and accurately, behavioral check lists should be developed. Figure 7–16 illustrates one checklist developed to train new instructors to use basic classroom presentation skills. This checklist was used during both practice and testing sessions. Your instructors should be given training on the administration and scoring of far-transfer tests. During rater training, several instructors score sample performances of varying quality. Consistency of scoring can be calculated by interrater reliabilities, a mathematical procedure available in most test design handbooks. After each independent rating, the criteria checklist should be discussed until all instructors interpret the criteria in more or less the same way. Each rating session should produce higher reliability scores. Because of the greater judgment required to evaluate application of principles, passing scores should be more flexible than with near-transfer types of training.

PREVIEW OF CHAPTER EIGHT

We have now looked at how to train all five types of content at the remember and use levels of performance. In the next chapter I will describe techniques for defining and organizing your technical content into courses and lessons. Then, in Chapter 9, I will look at some issues that apply only to computer-based training. This chapter will be of interest to you if you are designing CBT.

PART THREE

Organization of
Lessons and Courses

Putting It All Together: Organizing Your Training

CHAPTER SUMMARY

- Begin your training planning with a job analysis. A job analysis defines a job by describing activities in a top-down fashion, with functions at the highest level broken progressively into tasks, steps, and hidden mental skills.

- Functions describe major job responsibilities that are made up of several related tasks. Task statements begin with a verb and represent an activity that results in an observable job outcome. Near-transfer tasks are procedures made up of discrete steps. Far-transfer tasks are principle-based, made up of guidelines for action. Major lesson objectives are written at the task level.

- Hidden mental skills are facts, concepts, and decision criteria associated with all task steps that are unfamiliar to the target audience. They must be trained. Hidden mental skills already known to the trainees are considered prerequisites and will not be included in the training. Therefore you will need to do an analysis of your audience to decide what content will be considered prerequisite and what will be taught. Supporting learning objectives are written to describe acquisition of the hidden mental skills section of your lessons.

- After analyzing the job and the target population, you need to organize the content into a course. Courses are made up of chapters or units which in turn are made up of lessons. In general each lesson teaches one task and its associated hidden mental skills. When organizing the course, apply four major principles: zoom, common skills, spiral, and job-centered.

- The zoom principle recommends that you begin your course with a general overview of the content. As you move from one detailed chapter to another, review the overview to keep the learner oriented to the big picture. The zoom principle is especially important when learners are new to the content, and in CBT, where learner orientation needs extra attention from the course developer.

- Skills that appear redundantly on your task analysis because they are needed for many aspects of the job should be taught early in the course and then reviewed periodically in a spiral fashion. Thus, content should not be presented in a strict linear sequence. Advanced lessons should continue to reinforce earlier skills. This summarizes the common-skills-first and spiral principles.

- The job-centered principle suggests that you organize course content around job applications rather than around the structure of the knowledge itself.

- Organize each lesson following the structured format described in Chapter 2. Begin with an introduction and follow up with the hidden mental skills. If there are several hidden mental skills, add a practice exercise to insure they are acquired. After the hidden mental skills, teach the major lesson task, using the instructional methods for either procedures or principles, depending on whether the task is near- or far-transfer. Design practice to accompany the major task section of the lesson. End with a brief lesson summary.

- CBT lessons are organized following a similar pattern, except that there is more frequent insertion of practice to sustain attention and a final comprehensive practice to draw together all the lesson content.

- After completing the task analysis phase, summarize your training plans for management review and approval in a design document. Typical design documents include course and lesson outlines, learning objectives, a summary of instructional methods and media to be used, a sample lesson, a project management summary that includes timelines and resource requirements, and approval signoffs.

In the past five chapters I have summarized the instructional methods you need to teach each of the five content types at the remember and application levels. An introduction to structured lesson design in Chapter 2 suggested a generic model for lesson organization which includes four sections: a lesson introduction, background information, a target lesson task, and a summary. In this chapter I will describe in greater detail how to define the content of your technical training program and, having defined it, how to organize it into lessons and a course.

Although I have saved the discussion of how to define and organize content for the end of this book, you would actually undertake this work during the early stages of the instructional development process, primarily during the task analysis phase. See Chapter 1 to review the instructional development process.

HOW TO DEFINE THE CONTENT OF YOUR TRAINING

Because they have so much content knowledge, technical experts commonly make four errors when organizing lesson content. First, they organize the content around the structure of their expert knowledge rather than around the context of the job. Second, they fail to distinguish between content that is nice to know and that which is essential to the job. Third, they leave out important underlying information. Finally, they tend to cluster too much information together, neglecting to break it into short sections with frequent practice. The resulting courses tend to be packed with technical content that is not always job-relevant. In addition lessons often overestimate learner background and omit critical content. Learners can feel overwhelmed by a combination of missing information and too much information without practice. Many will assume the problems are theirs and end up demoralized and demotivated by the training experience. By building your training program on the results of a task analysis, you should avoid most of these pitfalls.

Focus on the Job

The first rule to guide your task analysis is: *Begin with the job.* Effective training for business and industry must help employees acquire the skills and knowledge needed to perform job-related tasks successfully. As illustrated in Figure 8–1, task analysis identifies the knowledge and skills required by the job, as well as what the target population already knows. Prior knowledge, subtracted from the job-required knowledge, results in the content of the training program.

Sort the content into an outline of lessons and units, applying several principles of organization to be discussed later. Then define what the trainees will do with the content by writing learning objectives. At the end of the process, you have a complete outline of each lesson in the course, as well as the lesson and chapter learning objectives.

The job analysis technique presented here assumes you are responsible for training an entire job. If you are only training a subset of the job, begin below the top levels. If you were designing customer service representative training for new-hires, you would be developing total job training. On the other hand, if you were

FIGURE 8–1 Defining Training by Job and Learner Analysis

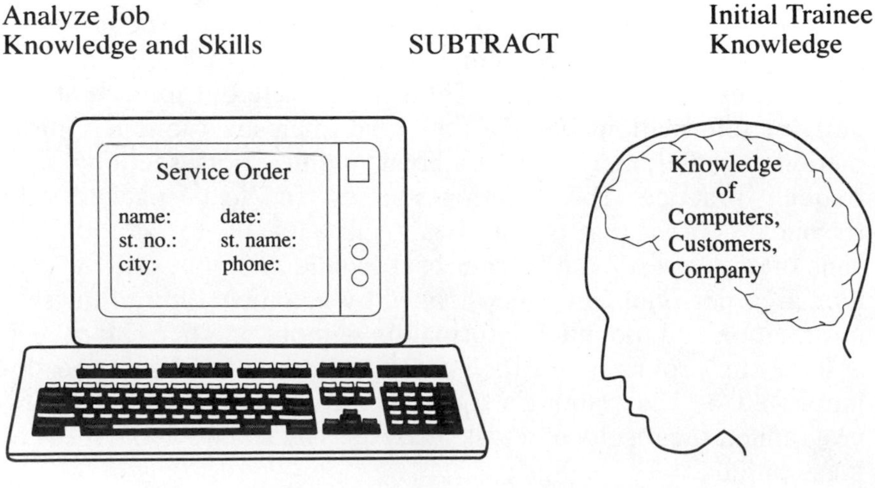

Analyze Job   Initial Trainee
Knowledge and Skills   SUBTRACT   Knowledge

responsible for training employees how to use the automated corporate interoffice mail and calendar system, you would be developing training for several tasks that might be associated with a variety of job functions. In either case, you need to begin with the job and organize your training around it.

This chapter has two major sections. The first describes a top-down technique for doing a job analysis. The second illustrates several principles for organizing your content into lessons, chapters, and courses.

ANALYZING THE JOB

A top-down process for defining the knowledge and skills associated with job performance includes defining job functions, tasks, steps, and hidden mental skills as follows:

1. Defining Job Functions

If you are training an entire job, begin by dividing the job into several non-overlapping functions. Job functions are similar to what your organization may call AORs (areas of responsibility), job duties, or KRAs (key results areas). In fact, you might be able to use as a starting point a job analysis which was already done for the purpose of performance appraisal or selection testing. Check with your personnel department to see if such studies have been documented.

A job function defines a major responsibility resulting in a specific output which is relatively distinct from other outputs. For example, customer service representatives working for a major utility handle a variety of customer telephone calls. Since the entire universe of their job is handling telephone calls, an effective way to define the functions would be by types of calls. Observations of and interviews with customer service representatives and their supervisors reveal four major types of calls: requests for service installations, questions about bills, requests for service repair, and credit inquiries from customers who cannot pay their bills. Figure 8–2 summarizes the major functional areas for two other jobs: inventory clerks and supervisors. Note that each functional area produces relatively independent job results.

FIGURE 8–2 Examples of Job Functions

Job	*Functions*
Utility Inventory Clerk	Transformer and Cable Inventory
	Customer Claims
	Payroll
	Street Light Accounting
	Facilities Mapping
Supervisor	Selecting Employees
	Providing Training
	Making Work Assignments
	Providing Feedback on Results
	Providing Appropriate Consequences
	Managing Employee Performance Problems

2. Defining Job Tasks Associated with Functions

Next look at each major job function (if you are training the entire job) and break it into several tasks. A job task is a job activity with a specific product. Completing the tasks associated with a particular function results in accomplishment of that function. Begin job-task definitions with a verb. There are a variety of ways to define the tasks associated with functions, none of them right or wrong. The major guideline is to keep the size of the tasks limited because they are the basis for lessons which should be kept brief. I'll return to the size issue in the next section.

Let's look at some of the functions described above and break them into tasks. One of the major functions of the customer service representative is handling service installation requests. Such a function can be broken down into tasks as follows: receiving the phone call, requesting and recording customer background information, establishing customer credit, and completing the call. These tasks as documented on Task Analysis Worksheet #2, illustrated in Figure 8–3. Figure 8–4 summarizes some of the major tasks associated with the payroll function of the inventory clerk job and the make-work-assignment function of supervisors.

FIGURE 8–3 Documentation of Service Installation Tasks

Lesson Author

TASK ANALYSIS WORKSHEET #2: TASK LISTS

Training Program:	Function:	Subfunction: (optional)
CUSTOMER SERVICE REPRESENTATIVE	SERVICE INSTALLATION	NA

Tasks Associated with Function:

Task: Receive the call

Description: Answer phone, greet customer, identify request

Task: Complete Customer Demographic Information on form

Description: Obtain/enter customer: name, phone, address,

social security number, installation address/date

Task: Establish Customer Credit

Description: Decide on credit deposit based on prior service

record, residence ownership, and employment

Task: Completion of Call

Description: Record deposit arrangements, verify information,

initial and route form

Task:

Description:

Task:

Description:

FIGURE 8–4 **Examples of Job Tasks Matched to Functions**

Job	*Function*	*Tasks*
Utility Inventory Clerk	Payroll	Complete Time Sheets
		Transfer Employees
		Document Rate of Pay Change
		Obtain Vacation Advance Pay
Supervisor	Making Work Assignments	List Department Outputs
		Define Experience Requirements of Each Output
		Define Time Requirements of Each Output
		Evaluate Experience Level/Motivation of Staff
		Organize Outputs into Tasks
		Divide Tasks Among Employees
		Define Expected Task Outputs
		Make Formal Task Assignments

3. Defining Steps or Guidelines Associated with each Task

Once you have identified the major tasks associated with each function you are training, evaluate each to determine whether they are near-transfer (based on a procedure) or far-transfer (based on principles or guidelines). If the task is primarily procedural, specify the steps that make up the procedure as described in Chapter 3. If it is far-transfer define the guidelines as described in Chapter 7. By documenting the steps or guidelines during task analysis, you develop the basis for the action and decision tables you will need for your training materials.

Limit the number of steps or guidelines to 15, in order to translate your tasks into brief lessons. The 15-step rule is a general guideline; you will have to make exceptions in some cases. But do limit the number of steps per task so employees are not overwhelmed with new information. If you are getting 30 steps, the task is probably too large. Divide it into two tasks. This will keep your lessons short and manageable. Employees with more experience can generally manage longer lessons with more complex information, but short lessons are necessary for trainees who are new to the content being trained and/or feeling a bit insecure about the training. Short lessons are important in CBT to sustain attention.

In the customer service representative job analysis, in Figure 8–3, the third task is *establishing customer credit*. Some of the relevant steps based on company credit policies and the automated system are documented on Task Analysis Worksheet #3, illustrated in Figure 8–5. Note that step statements begin with a verb and provide detailed job directions. If you write the steps in a directive format, you can convert them quickly into action and decision tables when you write your instructional materials. Thus, rather than writing for Step 1: Determine if the customer has prior service, a more directive phrase is, Ask the customer, "Have you had service with Reliable Utilities prior to this time?" The rule of thumb is that trainees should be able to follow the steps to successful task completion. If you have omitted steps or the step size is too big for the target audience, they will get lost. Your gauging of the level of detail will depend in part on the background knowledge and experience of the audience.

As you can see on the bottom of Task Analysis Worksheet #3, it is at the task level that you will define the major lesson objective. The major lesson objective requires the trainee to perform the task by following the steps or applying the guidelines presented in the lesson.

A far-transfer version of Task Analysis Worksheet #3, illustrated in Figure 8–6, specifies the guidelines associated with the define-work-assignment task of supervisory jobs. Note that the worksheet itemizes guidelines rather than steps, and includes an optional space to define the key task principle.

4. Defining the Hidden Mental Skills

Once you have broken tasks down into steps or guidelines, there is a final stage to complete the task analysis: identifying the hidden mental skills. The tasks and steps involve observable actions taken by employees; these are the how-to's of your training. However, to complete the tasks there are mental judgments or decisions to be made. For example, note that step 7 in Figure 8–5 states: "Determine if payment record is good or poor." To make this decision, the employee will need to know and apply decision criteria. Or suppose your task analysis yielded this step: "Obtain a duct thermometer." In order to complete this step, the employee would

FIGURE 8–5 Documentation of Steps Associated with Credit Task

Lesson Author

TASK ANALYSIS WORKSHEET #3: NEAR-TRANSFER TASKS

Training Program:	Function	Task#	Audience	Page 1 of 1
Customer Service Representative	Service Installation	3	New-Hire	
Task Name: How to Establish Credit				

Steps Associated with Task:

No.	Step Description
1	Ask customer, "Have you had prior service with Reliable?"
2	If yes, ask, "How long have you had service in your name?"
3	If no, go to step 8
4	Check "yes" box on form and access menu screen
5	On menu screen, select "Payment Record" and press enter
6	Enter social security number on "Payment Record" screen, enter
7	Determine if payment record is good or poor and check form
8	Ask customer, "Who is owner of this residence?"
9	Check "yes" if customer owns residence
10	Ask, "where have you worked and for how long?" — enter on form
11	Decide if deposit is required and enter on form

Task Objective

Given: simulated customer histories and access to computer system the trainee will: complete the credit portion of the installment form at a standard of: 100% accuracy

FIGURE 8–6 Documentation of Guidelines Associated with Define-Work Task

Lesson Author

TASK ANALYSIS WORKSHEET #3: FAR TRANSFER TASKS

Training Program:	Function	Task#	Audience	Page 1 of 4
New Supervisor	Make Work Assignments	3	new dept. managers	
Task Name: How to Define Work Assignments				
Principle: Make work assignments that are specific and challenging				

Guidelines Associated with Task:

No.	Guideline Description
1	Determine overall goals of your unit
2	Based on employee level, experience, motivation, determine appropriate time frame of assignments (daily, weekly, monthly, quarterly)
3	Based on employee level, experience, motivation, determine amount of discretion to allow (H, M, L)
4	Define expected work results appropriate to unit goals, time frame and amount of discretion
5	Write out specific expected results
6	Write out deadline date or time period
7	Write out the quality/quantity standards desired
8	Write out any special constraints
9	Schedule meeting to discuss work assignment
10	
11	

Task Objective

Given: a variety of unit goals and employee descriptions
the trainee will: construct work assignments
at a standard of: appropriate to guidelines provided

need to know two things: what a duct thermometer looks like, and where it can be located. These would be the hidden mental skills associated with that step.

Types of Hidden Mental Skills   Most hidden mental skills are of the following types:

- *Discriminations*. Will they know it when they see it? Discriminations involve knowledge of concepts or facts. For example, to use the duct thermometer, the trainee needs to know what a duct thermometer looks like — a concept. To fill out Form 6–13, the trainee must have the factual knowledge to identify it.
- *Factual Information*. What specific, unique knowledge is associated with the steps or guidelines? Appropriate factual knowledge would be required to answer the following questions: Where is the equipment located? What does credit code 5 stand for? Where is box 5 located on Form 3–19?
- *Decision Criteria*. If the task involves a branched procedure, the trainee will need to know the criteria which indicate a specific course of action. For example, on what criteria do I assign a specific credit code?

Hidden mental skills are the underlying facts, concepts, and decision criteria that often get left out of training programs designed by experts. To be sure you have defined all the hidden mental skills, you need to look at each step in the task analysis and ask yourself what concepts, facts or branched procedures might be there. Figure 8–7 shows Task Analysis Worksheet #4, listing the hidden mental skills associated with the steps for establishing customer credit. If there are several hidden mental skills, you may write a supporting lesson objective that describes what learners can do to demonstrate they have acquired them. The objective written at the bottom of the worksheet in Figure 8–7 states the outcomes associated with the hidden-mental-skills part of the credit lesson.

Defining Steps and Hidden Mental Skills: Knowing Your Audience

How small to make your step size and what to include as hidden mental skills depend both on the job to be trained and on the background knowledge of your potential audience. Prior knowledge and skills are prerequisites, and prerequisites will not be taught. In con-

FIGURE 8–7 **Documentation of Hidden Mental Skills Associated with Credit Task Steps**

Lesson Author

TASK ANALYSIS WORKSHEET #4: HIDDEN MENTAL SKILLS

Training Program:	Function	Task Name	Audience:	Page	of
Customer Service Representative	Service Installation	Credit	New Hire	1	1

Hidden Mental Skills Associated with Task Steps

Step No.	Hidden Mental Skills
1	What is prior service?
2	Must be 1 or more years in customer's name
3	
4	Location on form
5	What does payment record screen look like?
6	
7	Interpretation of payment record symbols — form location
8	Residence ownership counts as one criterion
9	Location on Form
10	Must be employed 1 or more years
11	If meet any of 3 criteria, no deposit needed — form location

HMS Objective: (optional)

Given: Screen printouts and customer background information
the trainee will: decide if a deposit would be required

at a standard of: 100% accuracy

trast, hidden mental skills are the underlying facts, concepts, and decision criteria supporting the task that your trainees don't yet know. They have to be included in the training program.

To decide whether the job knowledge and skills are prerequisites or hidden mental skills, you need to get a good idea of what your target audience already knows. You can interview sample target trainees or even test them to define their entry knowledge. If your trainee audience has varied background knowledge, you have three major alternatives:

1. *Design training for the lowest entry level of knowledge and skills.* If possible, provide this training separately for those trainees requiring it. Your course can be divided into introductory and advanced sections targeted toward the different entry-level skills of your trainees.

2. *Prepare pre-course work for entry level trainees.* Pre-course work can sometimes be used to equalize background knowledge. During planning for training on calculation of customer bills for experienced customer service representatives, all representatives were asked to bring their calculators. Pilot course sessions discovered that many of the representatives could not use them. Therefore, a pre-course worksheet required each participant to complete several mathematical problems using a calculator before attending class.

3. *Consider self-instructional training, especially for CBT.* You can tailor CBT lessons to meet the knowledge and skill needs of different audience backgrounds. Chapter 9 describes specific techniques for customizing CBT course content for audiences of varied backgrounds.

FROM JOB ANALYSIS TO COURSE AND LESSON OUTLINES

Once you have analyzed the job and target population and defined the functions, tasks, steps or guidelines, and hidden mental skills, you are ready to develop course and lesson outlines. Sequencing and combining the information defined in the job analysis into a course outline is a far-transfer task; there are no exact steps. This section summarizes four principles to consider when developing your course outline: zoom, common-skills-first, spiral, and job-centered.

The Zoom Principle

It is especially important for employees who are new to the information to get a broad picture of the target knowledge before getting the details. The novice needs to build a general cognitive framework in memory on which to attach or "hang" the details of the instruction. Once you have presented the big picture followed by some relevant detail, return to the big picture periodically to orient the learner and emphasize interrelationships. Reigeluth, in his *Instructional Design Theories and Models,* uses a camera analogy to illustrate this principle. As in Figure 8–8, begin the course with a wide-angle view capturing a broad picture of the content. Then zoom in on some detail. Before moving to a different detailed scene, bring the lens back out to the whole picture. This principle is especially important when your learners are new to the information and when your instruction will be delivered via computer. Because CBT screens cannot be accessed like book pages, special attention to orientation of the learner is needed.

Implementing the Zoom Principle   You can implement the zoom principle by starting with a process lesson or with an overview of content. If you were teaching maintenance of the components of the erylitizer, you might begin with an overview of the glopple generation process, relating it to the internal structures. If you were teaching the customer service representative job to new-hires, you could spend a chapter describing the process flow of work among the various functional areas in the customer service department, showing the interfaces between the representative and other departmental functions.

A second way to implement the zoom principle would be to begin the course with an overview of each major function or task to be trained. The new customer service representative should be presented with a general idea of the major types of calls he will be taking and how they relate to each other. Then, as the course progresses to detailed information on each call type, the big picture can be presented again periodically, giving even more detail on the interrelations between call types. If you were teaching employees how to use a new automated system, a broad picture of the major software functions could serve as a recurring focal point, allowing relationships of specific screens to the entire system to be built in

FIGURE 8–8 The Zoom Analogy of Course Organization

1. First give overview of whole course content at a general level.
2. Focus in on one part of the course in detail.
3. Return to big picture before moving on to the next part.

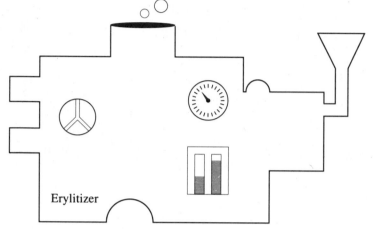

Erylitizer

1.   Overview of Erylitizer.

2.   How to read the hydropressure gauge.

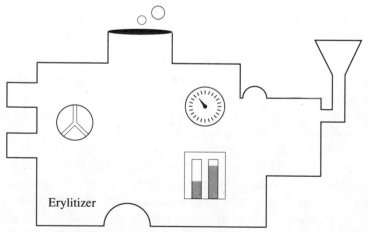

Erylitizer

3.   Relationship of gauge to whole Erylitizer.

memory. Figure 8–9 illustrates application of the zoom principle in a CBT course teaching the use of a specific query software.

The Common-Skills-First/Spiral Principles

These two principles complement each other. As you conduct your job analysis you will find certain guidelines, procedures, concepts, or facts associated with multiple functions or tasks. The customer service representatives use the telephone and computer in connection with every job function. Identify such reoccuring "foundation" content and teach it early in the course. For example, during the first week of customer service training, three basic skills are included: basic mechanics of the computer, mechanics of the telephone, and telephone courtesy techniques. Later, each of these foundation skills is reviewed at an increasing level of difficulty, as specific types of calls are trained. Such review of earlier skills reflects the spiral principle.

The spiral principle, illustrated in Figure 8–10, suggests that courses in general should not follow a strictly linear format. Instead, the foundation skills should be trained early and reinforced in more advanced lessons. Telephone courtesy provides a good example. The course begins with basic principles of good customer service. As each type of customer request is taught, courteous response techniques are stressed. The spiral principle recommends that a critical skill be presented at a general level early and reinforced at greater levels of complexity throughout the course.

BUILDING A JOB-RELEVANT KNOWLEDGE STRUCTURE

In addition to the principles described above, you can sequence and cluster information to be trained by following three organizational schemes: logical, knowledge-based, and job-centered. Let's look at each.

Logical Order

Some instructional content has very strong logical relationships in the knowledge itself; mathematics presents a dramatic example. Suppose you are teaching ways to solve simple linear equations in algebra. Before solving equations, the students must master addition and multiplication of negative numbers. If you are training content that has these strong internal prerequisites, you may not

FIGURE 8–9 Applying the Zoom Principle in CBT

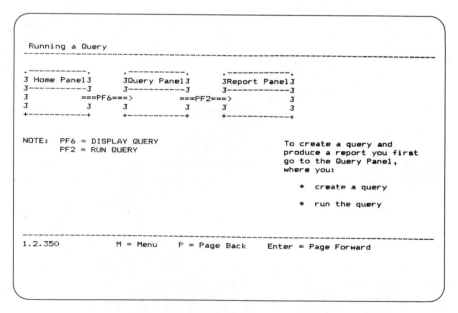

A.   Following a detailed lesson, an overview of screen relationships starts here.

B.   The overview picks up from Screen A and continues.

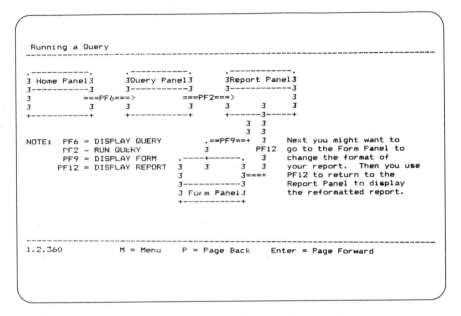

C.   This screen builds onto Screen B.

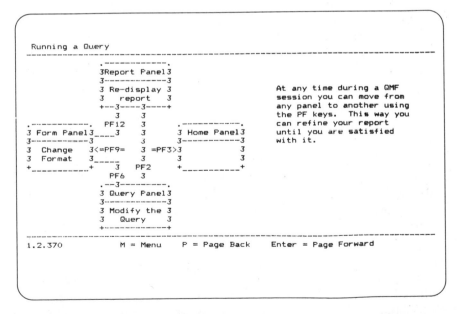

D.   The major panel interrelationships are summarized here.
Used with permission The Courseware Developers.

FIGURE 8–10 **The Spiral Principle of Course Organization**

THE SPIRAL CURRICULUM

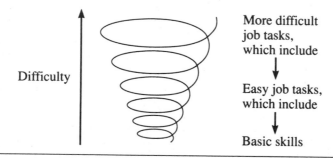

Difficulty

More difficult
job tasks,
which include

↓

Easy job tasks,
which include

↓

Basic skills

have much choice as to the content sequence. Skills A and B must be mastered before skill C. On the other hand, you may have content for which, from a logical point of view, there are a number of sequencing alternatives that would work. In that case, consider the difference between knowledge-based and job-centered organization.

Knowledge-Based versus Job-Centered Organization

Knowledge-based organization sequences and clusters topics around the structure of the knowledge itself. Most of our university courses are organized this way. A typical history survey course may start with ancient and progress to medieval and modern periods. A biology course will typically devote sections to zoology, botany, genetics, physiology, and other topics, based on the structure of the scientific knowledge. These knowledge taxonomies serve as the organizing force behind course structures. Often technical experts develop a complex and unique knowledge structure in their memory that may be taxonomic in nature. They will naturally tend to organize their courses in this manner.

By contrast, a job-centered organizational scheme will group knowledge according to how it will be used on the job. The job serves as the basis for the sequence and clustering of lesson material. Imagine a CBT course intended to teach foremen how to use a new automated inventory system to enter materials as they were installed or removed from the field. The training was designed by one of the programmers who developed the system. Quite naturally, the programmer organized the course content around his own mental view. Lessons focused around such topics as optional fields, mandatory fields, and error messages. The programmer did not spend any time with foremen and really had no direct knowledge of how the system would fit into their job tasks. It would have been better to develop a lesson on how to use the system when replacing a transformer or installing cable. Unfortunately the resulting CBT course was so out of the context of the foremen's jobs that they could not relate to it. The result of this training mistake was that foremen concluded the automated system was an unnecessary and irrelevant addition to their job.

Knowledge-based organizations are more related to far-transfer outcomes. In a university program, a general knowledge base is provided for lifetime access. Since university students are generally not preparing for any specific job, a more generalized educational approach is appropriate.

If you are going to be developing far-transfer training to meet specific job skill needs, build a job context as a structure to train the principles. A major semiconductor company is currently building a training program to result in a more principle-based understanding of the physics and chemistry underlying the production process. The target audience is the technicians who monitor the manufacturing operations. Currently, when problems arise they call on engineers. If engineering expertise is not available, production delays often result. The program hopes to provide technicians with sufficient understanding of the principles involved in their work so they can begin to solve some of the problems themselves. To be successful, it will be important to provide the relevant principles as they relate to the process operations. A pure knowledge-based course similar to college physics or chemistry will probably not provide the knowledge in a context that will transfer to problem solving on the job.

On rare occasions you might build a course almost solely on the structure of the knowledge. One of my clients designed training for engineers which was principle-based and lacked any specific job-related applications. The reason was both to improve morale and update general knowledge among engineers whose university expertise was becoming obsolete and who were expressing dissatisfaction with training opportunities. The investment paid off in greater employee satisfaction and, no doubt, in increased skill application as well. In this situation the corporate training organization assumed an educational rather than a training function.

To sum up, as you cluster and sequence the skills and knowledge you identified in your job analysis, apply:

- the zoom principle to keep trainees oriented
- the common-skills-first and spiral principles to move from easier foundation knowledge to more specialized and difficult content while incorporating the earlier skills
- the job-based principle to group most lesson content around the job-specific applications being trained.

Figure 8–11 illustrates a model course structure in which introductory chapters that present the common skills are followed first

FIGURE 8–11 Breaking the Course into Units, Modules, and Lessons

Organizing Your Course

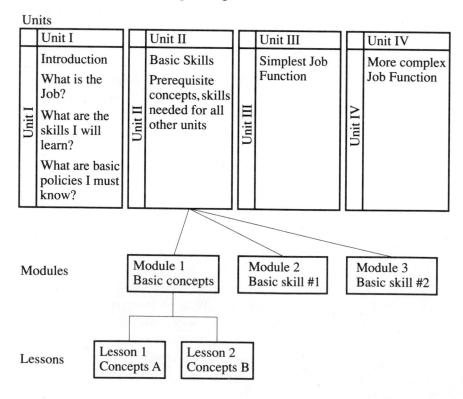

by chapters to teach the easier job functions, then chapters to teach the more difficult ones. In a fairly complex course such as this one, the units are broken into modules which are made up of several lessons. Otherwise the module level can be bypassed and units can be made up of lessons. Let's take a look at some guidelines for organization of individual lessons.

Principles of Lesson Organization

In Chapter 2, I described a structure for organizing individual lessons. As a general rule, your lessons should include an introduction, a section on the relevant hidden mental skills with an accompanying practice exercise, a major section on the core-task steps or guidelines with practice, and a summary. In classroom courses, practice exercises are essential after the major task section. If the hidden-mental-skills section includes several concepts, facts, or decision criteria, practice should be inserted there as well. Figure 8–12 illustrates an outline for a text lesson "How to Establish Credit," based on the task analysis presented earlier.

CBT lessons also include the general sections of introduction, hidden mental skills, major tasks, and summary. But the greater need for interaction requires frequent practice exercises inserted after every major chunk of knowledge. How large a chunk you present between questions depends on the experience of your audience. Novices need relatively smaller chunks with very frequent practice opportunities to process the new knowledge.

Outlines for CBT lessons are similar to those for texts, with a few exceptions. Figure 8–13 illustrates the outline for a CBT version of the same credit lesson outlined for classroom presentation in Figure 8–12. The expository screens present information using the display format guidelines described in earlier chapters. The practice screens require trainees to process the information just given at the application level. In general you should place practice screens after every idea chunk presented in the information screens.

One major difference in the structure of the CBT lesson is the placement of a separate practice section after the lesson summary. Since the questions throughout the lesson tend to be discrete, focusing on the information just provided, this final practice supports the achievement of the overall lesson objective. It is analogous to the practice designed following the major task section in the classroom lesson. If your lesson is procedural, this final practice might

FIGURE 8–12 **Lesson Outline for Credit Lesson: Workbook Version**

---

1. Introduction (1 page)
Now that we have obtained customer demographic information, we need to establish credit. This lesson describes credit criteria which will determine whether the customer must pay a deposit.

Credit is important to the customer because it determines payment of a deposit and to the company to offset write-offs . . .

Given Service Installation Form, simulated customer data, and computer system, you will determine whether the customer must pay a deposit with 100% accuracy.

Outline:
Lesson Introduction
Credit: Company Criteria Overview
What is Prior Service?
Required Screens and Forms
Meaning of credit codes and symbols for payment history
Practice
How to Establish Credit
Practice
Review
Quiz

II. Hidden Mental Skills (4–8 pages)
Overview of Company Credit Policy
Company Credit Criteria — rules for 3 criteria
What Is Prior Service? — 1 or more years service in your name
Recognition of Required Parts of the Form
Recognition of Screens needed
Meaning of screen symbols relative to payment history
PRACTICE 1 — 4–5 customer scenarios including screens — Do they have to pay a deposit?

III. How to Determine Credit from Payment History, Residence Ownership and Employment Data (4–5 pages)
Step-by-Step Follow-Along Demonstration
— How to determine prior service and payment record
— Obtaining information relative to residence ownership/employment
— Determining the deposit arrangement
PRACTICE 2 — Role-play nine customers with various credit criteria — complete forms and determine deposit need

be an unguided simulation. If your lesson is principle-based, it might involve a comprehensive case study, perhaps in the form of a simulation.

Summary of Lesson Sections

The Introduction   The lesson introduction is brief, but plays an important role in orienting and motivating the learner. In technical training we often forget to sell the benefits of what learners will achieve. Use the lesson introduction to be explicit about the value of the knowledge. Figure 8–14 shows the classroom-lesson introductory page for the credit lesson outlined in Figure 8–12. An effective lesson introduction should orient learners by explaining why they are learning this particular information, in terms of what they have just learned and what they are going to learn. It should clearly state the purpose and objective of the lesson, and motivate the learner by selling the lesson's benefits or importance. Finally, it should provide a preview of the lesson structure, with a lesson outline. Although most lesson introductions are fairly brief — contained in one or two pages, or four to five screens — they play a critical role by setting the stage for the lesson.

Hidden Mental Skills   The next section of the lesson should teach the hidden mental skills. Look at each hidden mental skill in your task analysis and decide whether it is a fact, concept, or decision criterion. Then use the formats described in Chapters 3–5 to display the required information and design practice. Figures 4–10 and 4–14 illustrate parts of the hidden mental skills section for the credit lesson. Teaching the hidden mental skills ahead of the major lesson task will offload the psychological burden of trying to perform a new task and master all the associated information at the same time. It will be easier for trainees to practice the steps to establish credit, once they already know the associated forms, computer screens, and decision criteria.

Lesson Task Section   The third section teaches the major task to be learned. Follow the rules for teaching procedures or principles with relevant practice exercises.

FIGURE 8–13 Lesson Outline for Credit Lesson: CBT Version

1. Introductory Frames
Title Frame—How to Establish Credit

Last session learned how to fill in customer background info

This lesson will focus on credit establishment

Important due to write offs and customer avoid deposits

If customer establishes credit, no deposit needed

3 credit criteria: prior service, home ownership, employment

Objective:

"You will be given customer information and asked to decide if the customer has to pay a deposit"

Lesson will take about 20 minutes

Add jump to summary option

2. 1st Hidden Mental Skill—Prior Service
Expository Screens

What is prior service—describe criteria and show form location

Practice Screens

Does this customer meet requirements for prior service?—3 questions

3. 2nd Hidden Mental Skill—Good Payment Record
Expository Screens

Show payment record screens and state meanings of symbol codes

Explain bullet rule

Practice Screens

Does this customer have good payment record?—5 questions

4. 3rd Hidden Mental Skill—Home Ownership/Employment
Expository Screens

Explain criteria of home ownership and employment rule

Practice Screens

Does this customer qualify via home ownership or employment?—4 items

5. How to Establish Customer Credit
Guided simulation through entire procedure

Shows how to access payment record screen and mark form

6. Summary Screen
Recap credit criteria and screen/form locations

7. Final Practice
Provide customer dialog and form

Trainee takes customer through entire credit establishment procedure and decides if deposit is needed. —4 unguided simulations

FIGURE 8–14 Sample Workbook Lesson Introduction for Credit Lesson

---

LESSON 3: HOW TO ESTABLISH CREDIT

Introduction   In the last lesson you learned how to solicit and enter the customer background information on the Service Installation form. This prepares you to complete the second half of the form which establishes customer credit.

Your effective use of the skills trained in this lesson is especially important to save our Company large revenue loss due to unpaid bills and to save credit-worthy customers the expense of a deposit.

Objective   You will be able to decide whether a customer must pay a $100 deposit when establishing his account to get service installed. You will need to be 100% accurate in following company credit policies.

Outline of Topics   This lesson will include:

Topics	Page
The 3 credit criteria	2
Prior service criteria	3
Computer screen symbols	4
Residence ownership/employment	5
How to determine deposit requirements	6

Lesson Summary   Last, a summary should encapsulate the major points covered and perhaps preview the material in the lesson to come.

Design Documentation

If your training program is of sufficient size, criticality, or cost, it is a good idea to put together an approval document, commonly called the design document, after you have completed the task analysis phase of your work. The design document summarizes the decisions you have made during task analysis on the four ingredients of instruction — content, objectives, methods, and media. It also documents relevant project management information. The purpose of the design document is to get all stakeholders in the training to agree on what is to be included, what outcomes can be expected, and all project details, *before* starting the development phase of your effort. Typical design documents include the course outlines, major instructional objectives, delivery plans, timelines and required resources, and instructional treatment sections. A sample lesson may also be included. CBT design documentation may include storyboards for one lesson, flow charts, or a prototype lesson.

PREVIEW OF CHAPTER 9

Up to this point, I have emphasized the similarities between development of training for CBT and classroom delivery. However, there are some major differences to consider when designing CBT. Chapter 9 will look at two of these: design of feedback, and tailoring of CBT for specialized audiences.

PART FOUR

Computer-Based Training: Some Unique Guidelines

CBT Versus Classroom Training: Some Design Differences

CHAPTER SUMMARY

- The focus on this book has been on instructional methods, not media. The instructional methods required to teach procedures, concepts, facts, processes, and principles are the same whether the instruction is delivered via workbook or computer.

- This chapter addresses two significant design differences in CBT: preparation of feedback, and tailoring CBT to meet diverse learner needs.

- Feedback is presented immediately following learner responses to questions indicating whether they are right or wrong and explaining why.

- Some guidelines for effective feedback design include: keep the question, learner answer, and feedback on the same screen; explain why each answer is right or wrong; give a hint and ask the learner to try again; tailor feedback to individual answers as much as possible; and use humor with caution.

- Simulations provide feedback in the form of natural responses of the microworld to learner manipulations. Instructional feedback can be added as well.

- A feedback table can save correct answers on the screen to provide a summary and memory-support vehicle.

- CBT can tailor training to meet needs of learners with varying backgrounds or trainees whose jobs require different types or levels of knowledge.

- Learner control refers to the amount of choice given to the trainee in the lesson. Control can be allocated over content or over instructional methods.

- More learner control is recommended when the learner population has greater background knowledge or higher aptitude, where there are few logical interdependencies among the topics, and when learning outcomes are to be measured.

- Adaptive control with advisement is a middle option between full and no learner control which has proved successful.

In Chapters 3–7, I described the instructional methods needed to train procedures, concepts, facts, processes, and principles. The instructional methods for each content type are the same for workbook and CBT; only the formats differ. For example, concepts require definitions, examples, non-examples, and analogies, whether delivered via workbook or computer. The differences reflect formatting differences between 8½"-by-11" pages and 80-line-by-20-column screens, as well as some constraints in design of practice exercises on the computer.

Despite these similarities, there are some significant aspects of CBT design not encountered in classroom training. In this chapter I will describe two of them: design of feedback, and ways to tailor CBT to meet needs of a varied training audience.

DESIGN OF FEEDBACK

Learning results from the processing of new information facilitated by effective practice exercises. I've stressed developing practice at the application level to ensure learning outcomes that are congruent with job requirements. Practice is so important that it should assume a top priority during your course development

FIGURE 9–1 Example of Effective CBT Feedback

Instructional Objectives   Practice 3

Type in the letter of the best instructional objective:

a. Given three credit summaries, you will circle all that meet
    credit criteria

b. You will know how to apply credit criteria to customer credit
    summaries

c. Given three credit summaries, you will mark all that meet
    credit criteria with 100% accuracy

> _____c_____

ABSOLUTELY — This objective includes a condition, action and
criterion statement. Let's try another question.

work. But practice is only effective when accompanied by well-
designed feedback.

In the classroom, the instructor provides feedback to the learners after the completion of practice exercises. In the development
of classroom instructional materials, a solutions page is generally
placed in the instructor's guide, and it is the instructor who judges
the accuracy of trainee responses and provides feedback. In computer-based training, there is often no instructor available. Therefore the developer needs to build answer analysis and feedback into
the CBT program itself.

Feedback is any response that informs the trainee of the correctness of their answers and explains why. Figure 9–1 illustrates
a typical correct-answer feedback message. A supportive comment
such as "*Absolutely*" adds a motivational element to the instructional message that explains why the answer is right. Research
shows that feedback is best when it is specific and provided immediately after responses.

Feedback for CBT is written in conjunction with answer analysis. In answer analysis, you define to the computer which responses are correct and incorrect. Answer analysis is easy for

structured-format questions such as dichomotous (Yes/No or True/False) or multiple-choice items. Answer analysis is much more challenging for open-ended questions such as fill-in or short-answer, as there are always several potential correct responses. You will need to identify most of them and build them into the answer analysis. Suppose the correct answer to your question is "Greater than two." You would program the computer to accept the responses of "Greater than two," "> 2," "Greater than 2," "> two."

In CBT you need to define the correct and incorrect responses, and to write feedback for each. Suppose your practice included a multiple-choice question with one correct and three incorrect answers. You would define which response is correct and then write four feedbacks, one for the correct answer and three different feedbacks for each of the three incorrect options. Since effective CBT should include many questions interspersed between information displays, development of feedback is a major task in CBT design. Typical estimates indicate that CBT takes three to four times as long to develop as classroom training. Certainly answer-analysis and writing good feedback accounts for a lot of that time. The next section will present some guidelines for writing effective feedback.

Guidelines for Design of Effective CBT Feedback

1: Keep Feedback on Same Screen with the Question   Take a look at Figure 9–2A, which displays the question, and B, which gives the feedback response. What problems do you see with screen B? These examples violate a basic rule of effective screen design for feedback. On the same screen the learner should see: the questions, the answer options, his answer choice, and the feedback. In Figure 9–2B neither the learner's answer nor the original question is visible. The learner must press enter to review the rules, at which point the question is gone. The screen design demands too much from human memory, which needs simultaneous access to all key feedback components. Figures 9–3A and 9–3B illustrate an improved version of these screens. In 9–3B the questions, answers, and feedback appear together. Note that the feedback message to the incorrect answer in 9–3B reviews the content.

FIGURE 9–2 Ineffective Screen Layout for Feedback

Database Design   Question 3

Which file Name(s) would be valid?

a.   3RDGYU
b.   A345
c. $rtfy
d.   file03

Type in letters of all correct file names: _____A_____

A.   Question Screen with Response

Database Design   Question 3

                              SORRY!!

Your answer was not right. Press enter to see the rules again.

B.   Feedback Screen for Question

FIGURE 9–3 Revised Screen Layout for Feedback

Database Design   Question 3

Which file name(s) would be valid?

a.   3RDGYU
b.   A345
c. $rtfy
d.   file03

Type in letters of all correct file names: _____a_____

Question Screen with Response

Database Design   Question 3

Which file name(s) would be valid?

a.   3RDGYU
b.   A345
c. $rtfy
d.   file03

Type in letters of all correct file names: _____a_____

NOT QUITE. Remember the name must start with an alpha character.
Look at the choices and try again . . .

Questions 9–5A with Feedback

2: Write Feedback to Verify Correctness and Explain Why. It's important, especially for incorrect answers, that the learner realize not only whether his answer is wrong, but also why. The feedback in Figure 9–3B tells the learner he is wrong and gives a reason. Write feedback for each wrong response that explains why that answer is incorrect. In this way feedback serves a teaching function.

3: For Incorrect Answers, Give a Hint and Ask the Learner to Try Again   In the feedback in Figure 9–4A the learner is told he is wrong and is asked to try again. However, without any additional help a retry is often frustrating. Better feedback to the same response in 9–4B tells the learner he is incorrect and gives a hint before asking him to try again.

There is no point in requiring a second try with dichotomous questions, since the correct answer is known by default. However, for multiple-choice or open-ended responses, rethinking an answer will increase the learning value of the question. A single hint and second attempt is enough. If a second response is still incorrect, chances are the learner needs more help and additional guessing will only result in frustration.

4: Provide a Correct Answer for All Questions in the Form of an Exit Message   In some situations the learner will not get the correct answer even with a hint and a second try. To be sure the correct answer is communicated, you need to write an "exit" message. Figure 9–5 illustrates a typical exit message for the instructional objective question. Exit messages are needed for all questions except dichotomous items, to provide for those who do not respond correctly even with hints and additional tries.

5: Tailor the Feedback to the Individual Answer as Closely as Possible   This is an easy guideline to implement for dichotomous or multiple-choice formats. For multiple-choice questions, build in feedback that tells why answer A is correct and why options B, C, D and E are wrong. However, what if you develop a matching question like the one illustrated in Figure 9–6? To developed a tailored response to all possible combinations of answers would require feedback for all possible combinations of the five options, a number that definitely exceeds productivity limits. What can you do?

FIGURE 9–4 Example of Incomplete CBT Feedback

Instructional Objectives   Practice 3

Type in the letter of the best instructional objective:

a. Given three credit summaries, you will circle all that meet
    credit criteria

b. You will know how to apply credit criteria to customer credit
    summaries

c. Given three credit summaries, you will mark all that meet
    credit criteria with 100% accuracy

> _____a_____

Sorry — Your answer is incorrect . . . Try again

Feedback Lacking Explanation

Instructional Objectives   Practice 3

Type in the letter of the best instructional objective:

a. Given three credit summaries, you will circle all that meet
    credit criteria

b. You will know how to apply credit criteria to customer credit
    summaries

c. Given three credit summaries, you will mark all that meet
    credit criteria with 100% accuracy

> _____a_____

A is close, but the performance criterion is not clear. Which choice has
clear standards of performance? Try again.

Feedback with Explanation and Hint

FIGURE 9–5 Example of Effective CBT Exit Message

Instructional Objectives   Practice 3

Type in the letter of the best instructional objective:

a.   Given three credit summaries, you will circle all that meet
     credit criteria

b.   You will know how to apply credit criteria to customer credit
     summaries

c.   Given three credit summaries, you will mark all that meet
     credit criteria with 100% accuracy

>   _____b_____

Your response is still incorrect. The correct answer is c because it
includes a condition statement, clear action and criteria. Let's review a
couple of examples and then try another practice.

FIGURE 9–6 Feedback Limitations of Matching Formats

Content Types   Practice 3

Match the correct example on the right with the content type on
the left:

____   Procedure   A.   Interaction supports learning
____   Concept   B.   How a tooth decays
____   Fact   C.   How to brush your teeth
____   Process   D.   Teeth appear around 7 months
____   Principle   E.   Decay

Depending on the capabilities of your authoring system, you may
be able to flag incorrect answers and ask the learner to correct just
those. Or you may have to give a global response such as "One or
more of your choices is incorrect. Try again!" If the answer were
still wrong, the exit message would display the correct matches.

Feedback for open ended questions also presents challenges.
Suppose you asked the question illustrated in Figure 9–7. The correct answers that should be built into the answer-analysis process

FIGURE 9–7 Answer Judging and Feedback for Open-Ended Formats

---

Motion Problems   Practice 3

A car is traveling at 50 KMPH. How far will it travel in 45 minutes?

>

A. Open Ended Questions Requiring Answer Judging

ANSWER ANALYSIS

Answers	Feedback
37.5	Great. You converted the minutes to hours to get the correct answer.
thirty seven and a half	Great. You converted the minutes to hours to get the correct answer.
37.5 km	Absolutely. You converted the minutes to hours to get the correct distance in kms
2250	Oops. Notice that the speed is in hours but the time is given in minutes. These need to be made equivalent. Try again.
22.5	You are incorrect but on the right track. 45 minutes is what proportion of 60 minutes? Try again.
UA	Your answer is not correct. Check the question and try again.
EXIT	You multiply 50 times 45/60 to get 37.5 Let's try another problem.

B. Some Possible Answer Judging for 9–7–A

include: "37.5," "thirty-seven and a half," "37.5 km," "thirty-seven and a half kilometers," and "37 1/2." But what about incorrect answers? The effective CBT author will anticipate the major mistakes and build them in with incorrect-answer feedback. In this problem, it is likely that some learners may not make the conversion between hours and minutes. Therefore the answer of 2250 might surface, along with others that reflect mathematical errors or lack of understanding of the principles. The major errors made should be anticipated in the answer analysis with appropriate feedback attached. Figure 9–7B shows the answer analysis for the mathematics problem illustrated in 9–7A. Note the UA (unanticipated answer) option. This is a response to be displayed prior to the exit message if none of the anticipated answers is received.

But how do you know what errors are likely to be made? Besides reasoning through likely errors, a good way to find out is to try the open-ended questions in paper and pencil format with a group of target learners. Evaluate all correct and incorrect responses and use them as a source of answer analysis and feedback. Of course, there is a productivity limit to identifying all possible answers. Therefore you will always need to write the exit message which provides the correct answer.

6: Word Feedback Positively; Use Humor with Caution   The feedback in Figure 9–8 was written to amuse. However it might be interpreted as insulting to some students. Use care with humor in feedback, and stress positive statements more than cynical ones.

We have covered six basic guidelines for design of feedback. Now let's look at opportunities for creativity in feedback design.

Creative Feedback Design

Designing Feedback in Simulations   In Chapters 3, 6, and 7 the simulation was presented as an approach to practice procedures, processes, or principles on the computer. In simulations, the real world is modeled in a miniature format, or microworld. The learner is encouraged to manipulate aspects of it, and feedback is embedded in how the microworld responds. This is a powerful form of feedback because real-world results provide tangible, immediate, and relevant knowledge. For example in the statistical control simulation illustrated in Figure 7–14, the learner could alter the process in several ways based on his evaluation of the control

FIGURE 9–8 Use Care With Humor in Feedback

Database Design   Question 3

Which file Name(s) would be valid?

a.   3RDGYU
b.   A345
c. $rtfy
d.   file03

Type in letters of all correct file names: _____A_____

It is suspected you are not paying attention . . . How many times have
we said you must begin with an alpha??

chart data. Suppose for example, the data points fell outside the upper control limits as illustrated in Figure 9–9. If the engineer chose option C, which is incorrect, the data points would continue to fall above control limits. The simulated response itself tells the engineer that this action did not solve the problem and prompts him to try another approach.

Adding Instructional Feedback to Simulation Responses   In addition to the simulation response of the microworld, you may want to add some instructional feedback as well. Instructional feedback can explain why the microworld reacted as it did or provide a hint. Figure 9–10 shows instructional feedback added to the simulation response in the process-control lesson. It is important to clearly show the instructional feedback as separate from the simulation itself. Using a box or consistent color for cuing is recommended.

In Chapter 3 we saw that when teaching computer procedures such as the use of application software, guided and unguided sim-

FIGURE 9–9 Feedback to Simulation

Principles of Statistical Quality Control   Simulation

Now that you have seen how to manage the quality process using control charts, let's apply the principle to a small process. Each time you press enter, a data point will appear on the control chart. You can take any of the actions listed below at any time and see the effect on the process.

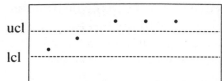

ucl

lcl

A.   Recalibrate micrometer
B.   Check input dimensions
C.   Realign die process
D.   Change vacuum pressure

ACTION DESIRED: ___C___

PF 1 = BACK   PF 2 = HELP   PF 3 = MENU   PF 4 = QUIT

FIGURE 9–10 Adding Instructional Feedback to Simulation Response

Principles of Statistical Quality Control   Simulation

Now that you have seen how to manage the quality process using control charts, let's apply the principle to a small process. Each time you press enter, a data point will appear on the control chart. You can take any of the actions listed below at any time and see the effect on the process.

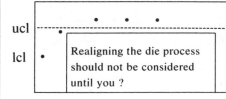

ucl

lcl

Realigning the die process should not be considered until you ?

A.   Recalibrate micrometer
B.   Check input dimensions
C.   Realign die process
D.   Change vacuum pressure

ACTION DESIRED: ___C___

PF 1 = BACK   PF 2 = HELP   PF 3 = MENU   PF 4 = QUIT

ulations are recommended for realistic practice. Your feedback can be of two types. First, you could provide system-based feedback in which the typical system message appears in the simulation. This might be a message such as "Enter numeric data only" if alpha characters were inadvertently keyed in a numeric field. You might also superimpose instructional feedback in a window, especially during early stages, to draw attention to the error. Figure 9–11B illustrates both instructional and system-generated feedback (DATE FIELD IN ERROR) to an incorrect response. As mentioned above, you need to use special care to keep the instructional message separate from the system-generated feedback.

When simulating operator entry into multi-field application screens, extensive feedback is often a challenge and may be impossible. If you anticipate software simulation to be a major application, carefully evaluate the ability of the authoring system to handle such simulations and to provide feedback. An alternative seen in Figure 9–11B is the use of positional feedback, where characters such as question marks appear in incorrectly filled fields. You can add instructional feedback in a window to further explain errors.

Combining Feedback in Summary Tables   To support memory, you can use a table to collect and preserve correct answers. The completed table provides a useful summary of information about the topics. For example, Figures 9–12A and 9–12B show a feedback table that saves responses to several related questions about features of different banks. As each question is correctly answered, the feedback box at the top preserves the answer. This builds an overview of this lesson section.

Effective answer analysis and feedback design are critical elements of CBT not encountered in classroom instruction. More in-depth discussions of design of feedback can be found in the CBT books cited in the bibliography. In addition, your authoring system should provide technical instruction for answer analysis, design of simulation feedback, construction of exit messages, etc. Along with design of feedback, CBT offers a second capability not available in classroom training: individualized instruction to meet diverse learner needs. Section 2 will address this issue.

FIGURE 9–11 Adding Instructional Feedback to Simulation

CSNTY — Unit A — Accounts Receivable
----

* * * * * * * * * * OPEN CASH DRAWER * * * * * * * * * * *
FILL IN APPLICABLE INFORMATION AND DEPRESS
ENTER KEY
                OPER — HOH   KAY — 11/29   TIME — 0413

  LOCATION — Torino   BATCH NO — 5252

  EFFECTIVE DATE — 11/29

> Complete this service order with the following information:
> LOCATION — Your office location is TORINO local office.
> BATCH NO — Your are authorized to use Number 5252
> EFFECTIVE DATE — Today is November 29, 1998.

PF 1 = BACK   PF 2 = HELP   PF 3 = MENU   PF 4 = QUIT

A. Simulation Question Screen

CSNTY — Unit A — Accounts Receivable

                                        DATE FIELD IN ERROR
* * * * * * * * * * OPEN CASH DRAWER * * * * * * * * * * *
FILL IN APPLICABLE INFORMATION AND DEPRESS
ENTER KEY
                OPER — HOH   KAY — 11/29   TIME — 0413

  LOCATION — Torino   BATCH NO — 5252

  EFFECTIVE DATE — ???? | DATE FORMAT MUST BE
                            | MONTH, DATE, YEAR

> Complete this service order with the following information:
> LOCATION — Your office location is TORINO local office.
> BATCH NO — Your are authorized to use Number 5252
> EFFECTIVE DATE — Today is November 29, 1998.

PF 1 = BACK   PF 2 = HELP   PF 3 = MENU   PF 4 = QUIT

B. Simulation Feedback with Positional and
Instructional Feedback

FIGURE 9–12 Saving Feedback to Support Memory

Section Five: Levels of Letters of Credit Security   Q1

Bearing in mind that the unconfirmed Letter of Credit has the guarantee of a bank in the buyer's country, for which of these situations would it be appropriate?

IRREVOCABLE UNCONFIRMED L/C	
Customer Risk	YES
Import Currency Control	
Sovereign Risk	

Is the unconfirmed Letter of Credit appropriate to protect against customer risk?
>   YES

Correct, the Letter of Credit is Suitable. The bank is guaranteeing payment, so the customer's pay status is unrelated.

PF 1 = BACK   PF 2 = HELP   PF 3 = MENU   PF 4 = QUIT

A. The Correct Feedback for Each Question is Summarized in the Right-Hand Corner Table.

Section Five: Levels of Letters of Credit Security   Q3

Bearing in mind that the unconfirmed Letter of Credit has the guarantee of a bank in the buyer's country, for which of these situations would it be appropriate?

IRREVOCABLE UNCONFIRMED L/C	
Customer Risk	YES
Import Currency Control	YES
Sovereign Risk	NO

Is the unconfirmed Letter of Credit appropriate to protect against sovereign risk?
>   NO

Correct, the Letter of Credit will not protect the selling party against situations of sovereign risk where the guaranteeing bank is also at risk.

PF 1 = BACK   PF 2 = HELP   PF 3 = MENU   PF 4 = QUIT

B. Use of Summary Table to Capture Multiple Responses

Reproduced by permission, Imperial Chemical Industries, plc. Design by Mantissa Computer Based Training.

USING CBT TO TAILOR TRAINING

Unlike classroom training, CBT allows you to tailor training to the different needs and backgrounds of a varied target audience. One challenge to all classroom instructors is dealing with trainees of diverse background, experience, and learning needs in the same class. There are few ideal solutions when the instruction is group-paced, as in the typical classroom. The instruction will be too slow for some, too fast for others. Or the topics will be too advanced for some, too basic for others. As a medium for providing self-instructional training, CBT gives the developer much greater flexibility to accommodate individual differences.

Tailoring and CBT: Two Case Studies

The Bank Case: Jobs Requiring Different Levels of Knowledge   A major bank entering a deregulated environment required new sets of skills for existing employees. To prepare for competition, all employees needed product knowledge and sales skills. As the front-line customer contacts, tellers needed basic product knowledge, introductory selling techniques, and awareness of internal product specialists for appropriate customer referrals. Loan officers, investment counselors and branch managers needed more in-depth product knowledge and sales techniques. In addition, some of the products were impacted by changes in tax laws which had important implications for customers. In this situation different job requirements indicated a need for diverse levels of training around a common set of product information and sales skills.

Management Training: Same Level of Knowledge Required from Diverse Learner Backgrounds   A second company established a structured curriculum which set competency requirements for all middle managers in preparation for advancement. One set of skills focused on financial management. Minimum competencies regarding financial analysis were established for all managers. The managers were from backgrounds as diverse as manufacturing, marketing, development, and finance. The finance managers already had substantial background in the course content and could probably meet competency requirements with little or no training, while other managers had varying levels of knowledge. In this situation, a common instructional outcome was sought from a population with diverse background in the target knowledge.

CBT solved both of these problems by allowing tailored instruction. To see how, let's take a look at the issue of learner control.

What is Learner Control?

Many recent conferences and popular articles on CBT have stressed the desirability of allowing the student to take charge of many aspects of the instruction. With learner control the student may choose what to learn and in what order, and perhaps whether to see examples or do a practice exercise. Although trainees generally like learner control, research shows that it is often is not a good idea from a learning perspective. A recent study showed that learner control gave poorer results in three out of four courses. In this section we will discuss various learner-control options, provide guidelines for use of learner control, and illustrate how to implement learner control in CBT.

What Can be Controlled?

Learner control can be provided in two domains: content and instructional methods. Let's look at each.

Control over Content: Figure 9–13 summarizes four content-control options. One form of content control allows choice as to what topics to take. John might choose topics A, B, and E, while Susan opts for D, E, and H. A second form of content control allows flexibility as to the sequence of topics. Bob might go

---

FIGURE 9–13 Learner Control over Content Variables

- Topics ABE or DEH
- Sequence ABEC or ECAB
- Level of Detail: overview vs in-depth
- Supporting information:
  notes, files, glossary, helps

FIGURE 9–14 Learner Control over Level of Detail: Flow Chart

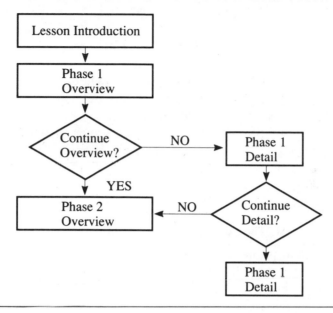

through the lesson in the order ABEC, while Susan chooses ECAB. If combined, these two options allow the learner to take topics in any sequence and skip any not wanted. A third form of control gives choice as to level of detail. Some programs might allow the learner to take the overview only or, at any point in the overview, drop down into more detailed explanation of content. The flow chart in Figure 9–14 illustrates the logic for a program offering control over levels of detail. A fourth type of content control gives optional access to supporting information in the form of glossaries, helps, or notes.

Learner Control over Instructional Methods   CBT also permits choice as to instructional strategies. For example, the student might choose the number or thematic context of examples. Suppose the course teaches ways to use a spread-sheet package to calculate a profit-and-loss statement. The target audience is managers in sales and production. The designer could build in several examples that use a sales scenario as context and several that fit a manufacturing theme, letting the student decide how many examples and which contexts were of interest. Trainees could also decide on the amount of practice they wanted, the difficulty levels, or the theme in which the practice was set. Other instructional methods that can be placed under learner control include the reading level, or the step size of the training.

The overall context of the instruction — whether it is presented in a tutorial or game format — can also be determined by learner control. Some adults prefer instruction in a game context, with scoring and competition against either the program or themselves. Many sales trainees prefer this type of instruction. Other populations prefer the more traditional approach of a tutorial with standard feedback. CBT could allow learners to choose the context they preferred.

The Learner-Control Continuum

Learner control is popular, but full learner control often doesn't work well instructionally, as many learners do not make the best decisions to meet their instructional needs. The learner control continuum presented in Figure 9–15 illustrates design options over learner control. At one end the learner has full control, allowing choice regarding content or instructional methods as described above. At the other end, full instructional control eliminates most learner options, with all trainees taking the lessons in the same

---

FIGURE 9–15 The Learner-Control Continuum

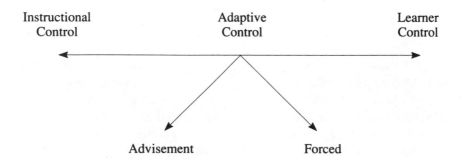

way. Pacing is the only major feature controlled by the trainee under instructional control, since most programs allow the learner to move through the program at their own rate.

Adaptive Control: The Best of Both Worlds?   Adaptive control provides a middle ground. Under adaptive control the options are managed by the computer, based on learner need. You program decision rules that tell the computer to adjust the instruction based on responses of the trainees. A typical adaptive control option adjusts the level of difficulty of sample problems. As illustrated in the flow chart in Figure 9–16, the trainee is given five problems of medium difficulty. If four of the five are answered correctly, the program either provides problems of greater difficulty or moves on to another topic. But if the trainee misses three or more of the five items, a decision rule will result in branching to simpler problems or to some additional instruction. Thus the instruction is adapted by the computer based on the accuracy of learner responses. For

FIGURE 9–16 Adaptive Control over Level of Difficulty: Flow Chart

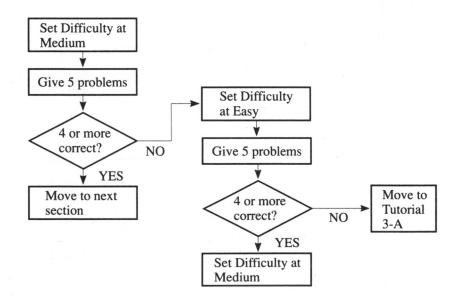

additional information see Section 3 of the Jonassen's *Instructional Designs for Microcomputer Courseware,* referenced in the bibliography.

Combining Adaptive Control with Learner Control: Advisement Adaptive control can be forced or optional. In forced adaptive control, the learner is automatically branched to the appropriate instruction, based on a decision rule embedded in the software. The learner has no knowledge of the rule or control over the program direction. But advisement can add learner control to adaptive control. In advisement the trainee is told how well he has done on the exercise and given an instructional recommendation. A typical advisement frame, illustrated in Figure 9–17, leaves the decision to follow or ignore the advice up to the learner. Research shows that when a criterion test is required to "pass" the course, either advisement or instructional control yield better results than learner control. However, most learners do prefer control options. This brings us to the topic of when and where to allow learner control.

FIGURE 9–17 Advisement Added to Adaptive Control

Database Design   Question 5

Which file Name(s) would be valid?

a.   3RDGYU
b.   A345
c. $rtfy
d.   file03

Type in letters of all correct file names: _____A_____

The correct answer is d since it follows all file naming rules. Since you missed 4 out of 5, it is recommended that you access Lesson 3–A for a review before continuing on.

FIGURE 9–18 Guidelines for Use of Learner Control

Factors Influencing Degree of Learner Control

- Prior knowledge of audience: low vs. high
- Learning skill level of audience: low vs. high
- Internal structure of content: low vs. high internal logic
- Criticality of knowledge and skills: low vs. high
- Motivation of audience: low vs. high

Guidelines for Learner Control
Learner Control should be

High regarding	When
Pacing through the Program Reviews, Back Paging, Helps	Always
Sequencing of Topics	Prior knowledge high Internal structure low
Choice of Topics Level of Detail	Accountability high, background knowledge varied, job requirements vary, advisement present
Level of Mastery	Skills not critical, training optional, advisement present

GUIDELINES FOR LEARNER CONTROL

As we have seen, your trainees can be given a great deal of control or almost none over the content or instructional methods. A fair amount of research gives us some guidelines for finding a happy medium. Figure 9–18 summarizes recommendations regarding when and where learner control will be productive. Two overriding factors are most relevant. First, consider the background knowledge of the target audience. If your learners are already experienced in the material to be trained or have high learning ability, greater learner control is recommended, since such learners are likely to make good instructional decisions for themselves. If your target population is new to the information or of average or lower learning ability, less control is better.

Second, consider the internal structure of the content. If there are strong interdependencies among the lesson skills, less learner control is recommended, especially for inexperienced students. That is, if you need to acquire the skills in lessons B and C before starting D, the learners should not have the option to skip B and C unless they demonstrate those skills.

There are some areas where learner control is always recommended. Pacing through a program is one. Except perhaps for an animated illustration, rate of screen display should be under learner control. This allows for different reading rates. All access to adjunct supporting information, such as helps, glossaries, or reviews, should be learner controlled. Backward navigation options including backpaging or returning to a marked section should be allowed.

FIGURE 9–19 Lesson Options for Bank Employees with Diverse Needs

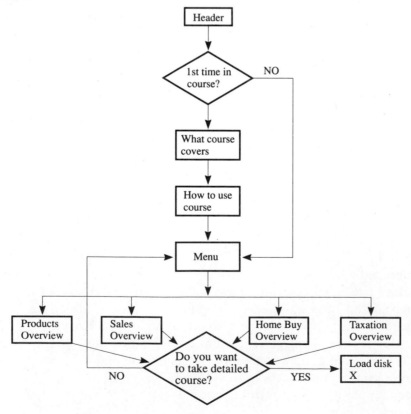

Two other major factors influence the amount of learner control provided. First, will a criterion test be required? If some demonstration of achievement of objectives is planned, then greater learner control can be allowed if supplemented with advisement. Since accountability is required to demonstrate competence, learners will be motivated to invest greater effort.

A second factor relates to the instructional development resources available. The more learner control, the more development work is involved. Earlier I described a learner-control option in which two contexts could be accessed to achieve the same outcome. The developer would need to provide two versions of the course which would add substantially to development time. During the planning process, decide how much learner control is desirable based on the audience to be trained and the cost and time constraints of the project.

To summarize, learner control is to be used carefully to meet specific business needs of the training. Because learners often do not make the best learning choices for themselves, full learner control is not recommended, except in pacing and perhaps for experienced learners.

Revisiting the Bank and Management Training CBT

Let's return to the two examples introduced at the start of this section and see how a program was tailored for each.

Bank Product and Sales Skills Training   The first situation involved bank employees whose jobs required different levels of product knowledge and sales skills. A flow chart of one solution to this problem is illustrated in Figure 9–19. Because the bank branches had PCs, the program was to be delivered on disks. The first disk provided a general introduction to the training and gave the learner the option to overview any of the product lines, basic sales techniques, home buyer guidelines, or taxation consequences. This disk was intended as full training for tellers and introductory training for higher-level personnel, giving them an overview of the topics to come and direct experience with targeted teller skills. Then a series of advanced-lesson disks were developed for the higher levels. Each advanced lesson began with questions regarding specific job responsibilities of the learner, then branched to a pre-test of the skills appropriate to those responsibilities.

Thus, sections on taxation implications for investment counselors would differ from those provided for loan officers. Each loan officer would only get the training indicated by his pretest.

Financial Training for Managers   In this situation managers had varied financial background and were all required to demonstrate a common competency level. The course developed a single program beginning with a pre-test, the results of which gave advisement as to which specific lessons were needed. Each lesson ended with a test which gave further advice as to mastery of the topic, including recommendations for optional resources if mastery was not achieved. The objective of this plan was to bring each manager to competency in the most efficient way. CBT allowed each manager to train in private on his own time to prepare for the competency test.

Techniques for Designing Learner Control

The flow charts in Figures 9–14, 9–16, and 9–19 illustrate some of the logic used to build in learner or adaptive control. This section will describe some screen designs that communicate control options to the learner. Figures 9–20A and 9–20B illustrate learner-control options in a software course. Note that the application screen in Figure 9–20A has six major sections. In this application each section is logically independent of the others. As the intended audience had varied experience working with earlier versions of the software, learner control was allowed. In this program, the learner is directed to choose which of the six sections to learn by typing an "X" over the "*" preceding each section. After "Enter" has been pressed, as you can see in 9–20B, the section selected remains in its original position, all other sections disappear, and a window is added, which provides instruction.

Allowing for Learner or Instructional Control   Figures 9–21A and 9–21B include two introductory screens from a CBT course on spread-sheet software. Learners can choose a beginner mode (9–21A), which offers little learner control, or an advanced mode (9–21B). The advanced mode permits considerable flexibility as to topics (e.g., setting-up versus formulas), instructional methods (overview or tutorial) and access to specific concepts (formulas, relative values, etc.).

FIGURE 9–20 Screen Design for Learner Control in Software Application

```
=== PROFILE =============================================== PAGE 1 OF 5 ===
                              * DEFAULT EDITOR MODES
1 LAST PAGE          |
2 NEXT PAGE          |   BASIC EASE Y   EDIT COLOR/      | VIEW MODE    Y  SELECT
3 QUIT               |   AUTOWRAP   N        GRAPHICS N  | OPTION MODE     ONE
4 COURSE CONTROLS    |   PF13 = PF1 N                    | EDIT MODE
                     |   NULLS      N                    |
-----------------    + ----------------------------------------------------
      DEFAULT        |              * DEFAULT START MENU
   EDIT WINDOWS      |
                     |   DEL/INS/WRAP/SPLIT Y    LETTER/CENTER    GRAPHICS
5 TEXT               |   WINDOW/MOVE/COPY        PUT/SAVE ....    SYMBOLS
6 FORM               |   BOX/LINE/FILL           COLOR .......
7 QUESTION           + ----------------------------------------------------
8 SIMULATION         |             * DEFAULT EDITING SYMBOLS
9 MULTIPLE CHOICE    |
                     |   HIGH ... >    HIGH INPUT ... !   HIGH MODIFIED INPUT ... (
-----------------    +  LOW .... <    LOW INPUT .... +   LOW MODIFIED INPUT .... )
                     |   MARK ... .    NULL CHAR .... .   PROTECTED INVISIBLE ... %
 * DEFAULT TABS      |   NEW LINE Z    NUMERIC    .... 9  INVISIBLE ............. X
                     + ----------------------------------------------------
1...+....1....+....2....+....3....+....4....+....5....+.,,,6,,.+ ...7....l....
      |              |         |         |         |         |         |
=============================================================================
```

A. To Learn About a Section, Trainee Types "X" over ""*
Note the X Next to Default-Edit Windows on Left Side

```
=== PROFILE =============================================== PAGE 1 OF 5 ===


                              +-----------------------------+
                              | THE DEFAULT EDIT WINDOWS     |
                              | SECTION LETS YOU DEFINE THE  |
-----------------    +        | DEFAULT WINDOW SIZE FOR      |
      DEFAULT        |        | EACH TYPE OF PHOENIX ITEM.   |
   EDIT WINDOWS      |        +-----------------------------+
                     |
5 TEXT               |
6 FORM               |
7 QUESTION           +
8 SIMULATION         |
9 MULTIPLE CHOICE    |
                     |
-----------------    +

1...+....1....+....2....+....3....+....4....+....5....+....6....+....7....+....8
```

B. Irrelevant Sections of Screen Disappear;
Instructional Window is Added

Screens were developed using the PHOENIX® System from Goal Systems, International, Inc.

FIGURE 9–21 Screen Design for High and Low Learner Control Options

Introduction to Spreadsheet Software
 	
Beginner Mode
	Take each lesson in the order shown on the menu:
	
	    A. Introduction to Course
	    B. Overview of Spreadsheet Software
	    C. Setting Up Your Spreadsheet
	    D. Inserting Formulas
	    E. Relative and Absolute Values
	    F. Advanced Topics

A. Beginner Mode: Provides Structured Menu Approach

Introduction to Spreadsheet Software Advanced Mode	Choose the Topic and Section You Want TOPIC OVERVIEW TUTORIAL PRACTICE Use of Software Setting Up Formulas Budget Setups Projections Choose any concept you want explained Submenus will give more options	 formulas relative values absolute values advanced functions

B. Advanced Mode: Allows Access in any Order by Topic or by Choosing Individual Terms

Intelligent Tutors: The future of CBT   A number of research projects have designed instruction using artificial-intelligence systems. These so-called "intelligent tutors" solve the problem of learner control by acting like human tutors. Rather than relying on preprogrammed instructional strategies, the system dynamically builds a model of the learner based on responses to the program. This model then interfaces with an instructional model which can provide the learner with the most appropriate instructional strategies when and where needed. At this point these systems are not practical for widespread commercial application. For more information see Polson and Richardson's *Intelligent Tutoring Systems,* referenced in the bibliography.

Learner Control: Summary

This section has provided some guidelines on when to use, and how to implement various learner-control options. Learner control, especially with advisement offers great potential to the age-old challenge of efficiently meeting diverse learning needs. At the same time, research shows that full learner control often yields suboptimal instructional outcomes and requires greater instructional overhead. Use learner control judiciously, applying the guidelines in this chapter.

Appendixes

Appendix I: Exercises

Solutions appear on the pages following each exercise

EXERCISE FOR CHAPTER 1

The Four Ingredients of Training

Read the brief instructional development scenario below and, on a piece of paper, make four lists to identify the information or content, performance outcome, instructional methods, and instructional media of this program.

Diane plans to teach a refresher class to experienced sales representatives at Optical Scientific Products on how to best close a sale. She spends a month observing and interviewing effective and less effective account representatives, noting similarities and differences in how they handle their sales calls. She summarizes five steps used by the best representatives that are not used by the less effective performers.

Diane summarizes the five steps in a list on a card to be used during and after the training for reference on the job. Then she videotapes several examples of the five steps in various customer situations to be used during class to illustrate different approaches. Diane writes out some role-playing scenarios for classroom practice to be administered and critiqued by the instructors.

EXERCISE FOR CHAPTER 1: SOLUTIONS

The Four Ingredients of Training

Information or content:
   The five steps for closing the sale.

Performance Outcome:
   Given a series of simulated account-representative–customer in-
   teractions and the job card, you will apply the five steps to close
   the sale.

Instructional Methods:
Informational Methods:
   List–of 5 steps
   Examples of application of 5 steps.
Practice Methods:
   Role-play
   Applying the five steps with instructor feedback.

Instructional Media:
   Instructor, video, card

Comments:
   The *media* deliver the instructional methods. In this situation the
video will deliver the examples, the job card the list of five steps,
and the instructor the practice and feedback.
   The *instructional methods* are techniques used to cause learning.
They are informational and practice. In this situation the five steps
are presented in a list supplemented by examples illustrating their
application. The practice methods are role playing with feedback.
   The *content,* or information, of the program is the five steps
needed to close the sale, derived through observation of expert
performance.
   The *performance outcome* states what the learners will do at the
end of the class to demonstrate they have acquired the content. In
this case they will need to apply the five steps to the close of a sale.

EXERCISE FOR CHAPTER 3

Distinguishing Between Linear and Branched Procedures

For each procedure listed below, indicate whether it is linear or branched.

1. How to repair the malfunctioning copy machine.
2. How to approve or disapprove a customer order.
3. How to calculate the standard deviation.
4. How to determine charge based on quality and quantity of customer order.
5. How to use the search-and-replace command.
6. How to compute the customer's car insurance rate.
7. How to replace the printer cartridge.

EXERCISE FOR CHAPTER 3: SOLUTIONS

Distinguishing Between Linear and Branched Procedures

1. Branched, assuming there are clear-cut troubleshooting steps of the if-X-symptom-appears then-do-Y variety.

2. Branched, assuming there are specific criteria for approval and disapproval.

3. Linear. A single series of action steps can be specified to do this calculation.

4. Branched. Customer charges would be based on specific criteria regarding quality and quantity of purchase.

5. Linear. A single series of action steps can be described for this procedure.

6. Branched. Many criteria regarding type of car, driver age, driving record, etc. would guide this procedure.

7. Linear. A single series of steps makes up this procedure.

Comments:

The assumptions stated above regarding criteria are what determine the answers. If you made different assumptions based on your experience, don't worry. The main idea here is to distinguish between procedures that involve a single set of steps and those that provide defined criteria for following any of several action sequences.

EXERCISE FOR CHAPTER 4

Identifying Concepts

The following sentences are steps or guidelines for completing various technical tasks. For each sentence, list on a piece of paper any concepts mentioned.

1. Assemble the duct thermometer and ladder.
2. Locate the supply air register in the ceiling.
3. Enter all normal and overtime worked.
4. Distinguish metamorphic from sedimentary deposits.
5. Make an empathetic response.

EXERCISE FOR CHAPTER 4: SOLUTIONS

Identifying Concepts

1. duct thermometer and ladder
2. supply air register and ceiling
3. normal and overtime
4. metamorphic and sedimentary deposits
5. empathetic response

Comments:

Recall that a concept represents a class of things called by a common name. Members of the class share common features and vary on irrelevant features. If there are multiple examples, you are dealing with a concept.

In these examples we see a mix of concepts, some more technical and some common.

1.   "Duct thermometer" is a technical concept. To perform this step the employee would need to distinguish it from other thermometers. By contrast, "ladder" is an everyday concept.

2.   Supply air registers need to be distinguished from other vents in the ceiling. "Ceiling" is another everyday concept.

3.   To enter normal and overtime you would need to know how they are defined by the company.

4.   There are multiple different examples of metamorphic and sedimentary deposits.

5.   An empathetic response could involve a variety of phrases, any of which would qualify as empathetic.

EXERCISE FOR CHAPTER 5

Distinguishing Between Facts and Concepts

This exercise assumes you have read both Chapters 4 and 5. For each instructional task below, indicate whether the italicized supporting information should be treated as a concept or as a fact.

1. How to use the *special function keys* to access needed information in the new computer software.

2. How to respond to the angry customer with *empathy*.

3. How to calculate a *standard deviation*.

4. How to replace the *Model 4–50 printer cartridge*.

5. How to fill out the *company timesheet*.

6. How to enter customer data on the *order-entry computer screen*.

7. How to tell the customer the *telephone number of his local office*.

8. How to enter all *normal time* worked on the timesheet.

EXERCISE FOR CHAPTER 5: SOLUTIONS

Distinguishing Between Facts and Concepts

1. Fact. In order to complete this task you would need to know the specific capabilities of each function key. Since this is one-of-a-kind information, it would be factual.

2. Concept. Since there are a variety of examples of empathy, it would be a concept.

3. Concept. Standard deviation is a concept, since you can define it and show multiple different examples.

4. Fact. Because this involves a unique, specific piece of equipment, this is an example of factual information.

5. Fact. Assuming the company uses a unique, specific form as a timesheet, each one would look like every other, and thus be an example of factual information.

6. Fact. Assuming each order-entry screen is identical to every other one, this would be factual.

7. Fact. Each telephone number is unique and specific.

8. Concept. There are multiple different examples of normal time worked. To identify normal time you would need a definition to apply to the various examples.

EXERCISE FOR CHAPTER 6

Identifying Processes

Indicate which of the examples below are procedural tasks and which are processes. For each process, *indicate if it is business or technical.*

1. How to fill out your college application form.
2. How the university admits new freshmen.
3. How the laser printer works.
4. How to replace the printer cartridge.
5. How the computer program sorts data.
6. How to set up a spread sheet.
7. How data processing designs and develops new software products.
8. How to code the GEN = MAP macro.
9. How DNA replicates.

EXERCISE FOR CHAPTER 6: SOLUTIONS

Identifying Processes

1. Procedure: since a single individual could complete this task, it is not a process.

2. Process. Business: college admission includes a variety of individuals involved in selection and administration of applicants.

3. Process. Technical: describes stages in a mechanical system.

4. Procedure: a task that a single individual could complete.

5. Process. Technical: describes stages in an electronic system.

6. Procedure: a task that a single individual could complete.

7. Process. Business: various analysts, programmers, and the client are involved in software design and development.

8. Procedure: a single individual could do this.

9. Process. Technical: describes stages in a natural system.

Comments:

Tasks are activities that a single individual could accomplish. Procedural tasks tell the employee how to do something. By contrast, processes tell employees how things work; they are systems in action beyond the control of any one individual. You cannot train an individual to do a process—only about how the process works. Note that business processes involve a series of procedures completed by different individuals.

EXERCISE FOR CHAPTER 7

Distinguishing Between Near- and Far-Transfer Tasks

For each task below, write N or F to indicate whether it fits more into the category of near- or far-transfer.

1. Changing a tire.
2. Making a sale.
3. Teaching a course.
4. Coding in COBOL.
5. Doing a blood count.
6. Calculating the standard deviation.
7. Filling out a timesheet.
8. Flying the L–1011.
9. Establishing customer credit.
10. Assigning employees work tasks.

EXERCISE FOR CHAPTER 7: SOLUTIONS

Distinguishing Between Near- and Far-Transfer Tasks

1. Near-transfer. This is a procedure based on steps.

2. Far-transfer. Each sale will be different depending on the customer and product. Guidelines are needed here.

3. Far-transfer. Experienced instructors know that no two classes are ever taught the same way. Each class has unique needs.

4. Near- and far-transfer. While the syntax may be clear-cut and thus near-transfer, programmers tell me that while several programs can achieve the same result, some are much more efficient than others. They say program design is far-transfer.

5. Near-transfer. This is a procedure.

6. Near-transfer. The calculation can be accomplished by applying a series of steps which would be followed the same way each time.

7. Near-transfer. Assuming a specific timesheet, a procedure can be applied to fill it out.

8. Near- and far-transfer. Pilots tell me that routine flying is near-transfer, like driving a car; but, when the unexpected comes up, considerable pilot judgment is needed.

9. Near-transfer. This is an example of a branched procedure. Assuming there are specific criteria to follow to establish credit, there would be clear steps to follow.

10. Far-transfer. Effective work assignments would vary depending on the goals of the organization and specific employee levels and experience.

Appendix II: Training Resources for Developing Instructional Materials

Company	Training	Contact
Clark Training Consulting	Instructional Development Workshop for Technical Experts	(213) 541-3321
	Classroom Management Workshop for Technical Experts	
Information Mapping® (R.E. Horn)	Writing Procedures, Policies and Documentation	(617) 890–7003
	Writing Management Reports	
	Developing Effective Computer Documentation	
	How to Design, Develop, and Evaluate CBT	
Robert Mager	Criterion-Referenced Instruction	(404) 458–4080
	Instructional Module Development	
	Classroom Presentation Skills	
Darryl Sink & Associates	Instructional Design	(408) 272–8384

Appendix III: Professional Organizations

Organization	Focus	Contact
National Society for Performance and Instruction (NSPI)	Performance Improvement • Instructional Design • Non-instructional interventions	(202) 861–0777
American Society for Training and Development (ASTD)	Training and Human Resource Development	(703) 683–8171

Instructional Design References

These references are not intended to be exhaustive. I have included specific citations mentioned in the text and additional recent books and articles relating to the topics discussed. You can access older resources by referring to the bibliographies of these recent works.

INSTRUCTIONAL SYSTEMS DESIGN (GENERAL)

Gagne, R. M., ed. 1987. *Instructional technology foundations.* Hillsdale, NJ: Lawrence Erlbaum.

Gagne, R. M., L. J. Briggs, and W. W. Wager 1988. *Principles of instructional design.* New York: Holt, Rinehart and Winston.

Goldstein, R. L. 1986. *Training in organizations: Needs assessment, development, and evaluation* (2nd ed.). Monterey, CA: Brooks/Cole.

Kearsley, G. 1984. *Training and technology: A handbook for HRD professionals.* Reading, MA: Addison-Wesley.

Kemp, J. 1985. *The instructional design process.* New York: Harper & Row.

Reigeluth, C. M., ed. 1983. *Instructional design theories and models.* Hillsdale, NJ: Lawrence Erlbaum.

Reigeluth, C. M., ed. 1987. *Instructional theories in action.* Hillsdale, NJ: Lawrence Erlbaum.

Schiffman, S. S. 1986. Instructional systems design: Five views of the field. *Journal of instructional development* 9 (3): 14–21.

NEEDS ASSESSMENT/TASK ANALYSIS

Cantor, J. A. 1986. The Delphi as a job analysis tool. *Journal of instructional development* 9 (1): 16–19.

Carlisle, K. E. 1986. *Analyzing jobs and tasks.* Englewood Cliffs, NJ: Educational Technology.

Edwards, B., P. Fiore, and J. Van Lare. 1984. *Conducting the training needs analysis.* 1984. New York: Training by Design.

Jonassen, D. H., and W. Hannum. 1986. Analysis of task analysis procedures. *Journal of instructional development* 9 (2): 2–12.

Mager, R., and P. Pipe. Analyzing performance problems.

Rodriguez, S. R. 1988. Needs assessment and analysis: Tools for change. *Journal of instructional development* 11 (1): 23–27.

Rossett, A. 1987. *Training needs assessment.* Englewood Cliffs, NJ: Educational Technology.

Wedman, J. F. 1987. Task analysis: Conceptualizing unfamiliar content. *Journal of instructional development* 9 (1): 16–19, 10 (3): 16–21.

Zemke, R., and T. Kramlinger. 1982. *Figuring things out: A trainer's guide to needs and task analysis.* Reading, MA: Addison-Wesley.

LEARNING OBJECTIVES

Mager, R. 1975. *Preparing instructional objectives* (2nd Ed.). Belmont, CA: Fearon.

DEVELOPMENT OF INSTRUCTION

General

Clark, R. 1986. Defining the D in ISD, part 1: Task-general instructional methods. *Performance & instruction* 25 (1): 17–21.

Clark, R. 1986. Defining the D in ISD, part 2: Task-specific instructional methods. *Performance & instruction* 25 (3): 12–17.

Merrill, M. D. 1987. A lesson based on the component display theory. In Reigeluth, C. M., ed. *Instructional theories in action lessons illustrating selected theories and models.* Hillsdale, NJ: Lawrence Erlbaum.

Merrill, M. D. 1983. Component display theory. In Reigeluth, C. M., ed. *Instructional design theories and models.* Hillsdale, NJ: Lawrence Erlbaum.

Concepts

McCallum, D., A. Apking, and D. Snyder. 1987. Design tactics for using examples: A reader participation article. *Performance & instruction* 26 (9): 37–45.

Newby, T. J., and D. A. Stepich. 1987. Learning abstract concepts: The use of analogies as a mediational strategy. *Journal of instructional development* 10 (2): 20–26.

Tennyson, R. D., and M. J. Cocchiarella. 1986. An empirically based instructional design theory for teaching concepts. *Review of educational research* 56 (1): 40–71.

Wilson, B. 1986. What is a concept? Concept teaching and cognitive psychology. *Performance & instruction* 25 (10): 16–18.

Yelon, S., and A. Winerman. 1987. Efficient lesson development. *Performance and instruction* 26 (6): 1–6.

Yelon, S., and M. Massis. 1987. Heuristics for creating examples. *Peformance & instruction* 26 (8): 13–17.

Procedures

Wilson, B. G. 1985. Techniques for teaching procedures. *Journal of instructional development* 8 (2): 2–5.

Practice

Salisbury, D. F., B. F. Richards, and J. D. Klein. 1985. Designing practice: A review of prescriptions and recommendations from instructional development theories. *Journal of instructional development* 8 (4): 9–19.

Analogies

Johsua, S., and J. J. Dupin. 1987. Taking into account student conceptions in instructional strategy: An example in physics. *Cognition and instruction* 4 (2): 117–35.

Text Design

Harley, J., and J. Trueman. 1985. A research strategy for text designers: The role of headings. *Instructional science* 14: 99–155.

Horn, R. E. 1982. Structured writing and text design. In D. H. Jonassen, ed. *The technology of text*. Englewood Cliffs, NJ: Educational Technology.

Kiewra, K., and G. M. Frank. Encoding and external storage effects of personal lecture notes, skeletal notes, and detailed notes for field independent and field dependent learners. *Journal of educational research*.

Streit, L. D., S. Stern, and R. H. Collins. 1986. Managing training materials with structured text design. *Performance & instruction* 25 (1): 10–13.

EVALUATION

Berk, R. A., ed. 1986. Performance assessment: Methods and applications. Baltimore: Johns Hopkins.

Gronlund, N. E. 1981. *Measuring educational outcomes: Fundamentals of testing* (4th ed.). New York: Macmillan.

Shrock, S. A., and W. C. Coscarelli. 1989. *Criterion-referenced test development: Technical and legal guidelines for corporate training.* Reading, MA: Addison-Wesley Publishing Company, Inc.

Shrock, S., R. Mansukhami, W. Coscarelli, and S. Palmer. 1986. An overview of criterion-referenced text development. *Performance & instruction* 25 (6): 3.

COMPUTER-BASED TRAINING

Alessi, S. M., and S. Trollip. 1985. *Computer based instruction: Methods and development.* Englewood Cliffs, NJ: Prentice-Hall.

Allred, K. F., and C. Locatis. 1988. Research, instructional design, and new technology. *Journal of instructional development* 11 (1): 2–5.

Clark, R. 1989. Who's in control. *CBT directions.* February 6–7, 1989.

Gery, G. 1987. *Making CBT happen.* Boston, MA: Weingarten.

Jonassen, D. H., ed. 1988. *Instructional designs for microcomputer courseware.* Hillsdale, NJ: Lawrence Erlbaum.

Kearsley, G. 1986. *Authoring: A guide to the design of instructional software.* Reading, MA: Addison-Wesley Publishing Company, Inc.

Kincaid, J. P., R. Braby, and J. E. Mears. 1988. Electronic authoring and delivery of technical information. *Journal of instructional development* 11 (2): 8–13.

Laurillard, D. 1987. Computers and the emancipation of students: giving control to the learner. *Instructional science* 16: 3–18.

Merrill, M. D. 1988. Applying component display theory to the design of courseware. In Jonassen, D. H., ed. *Instructional designs for microcomputer courseware.* Hillsdale, NJ: Lawrence Erlbaum.

Merrill, M. D. 1987. The new component design theory: instructional design for courseware authoring. *Instructional science* 16: 19–34.

Morrison, G. R., and S. M. Ross. 1988. A four stage model for planning computer based instruction. *Journal of instructional development* 11 (1): 6–14.

Polson, M. C., and J. J. Richardson, eds. 1988. *Intelligent tutoring systems.* Hillsdale, NJ: Lawrence Erlbaum.

Reiser, R., and R. M. Gagne. 1983. *Selecting media for instruction.* Englewood Cliffs, NJ: Educational Technology.

Index